Parenting 20-Something KIDS

Recognizing Your Role as They Find Their Way

MARTHA POPE GORRIS

Beacon Hill Press of Kansas City
Kansas City, Missouri

ISBN 083-412-2243

Printed in the
United States of America

Cover Design: Darlene Filley

Library of Congress Cataloging-in-Publication Data

Gorris, Martha Pope, 1949-
Parenting 20-something kids : recognizing your role as they find their way / Martha Pope Gorris.
p. cm.
Includes bibliographical references (p.   ).
ISBN 0-8341-2224-3 (pbk.)
1. Parenting—Religious aspects—Christianity. 2. Parent and adult child—Religious aspects—Christianity. I. Title.

BV4529.G67 2005
248.8'45—dc22

2005023308

10 9 8 7 6 5 4 3 2 1

Contents

Introduction

AS I write this, my daughters are on their own, ages 28 and 25. Graduating from graduate school and college respectively, they decided last year to move to Hawaii. Our older daughter had a developing love interest there, and our younger daughter—well, Meg simply got caught up in the excitement of moving to paradise. Today both young women are settled in their jobs, enjoying being Hawaiian locals.

It was in the process of helping them get to Hawaii that we made new realizations that our parenting role was changing in other ways. Talking over their plans, helping them move out of their apartments, sorting through what stays, what goes, and what will remain in storage for the "duration" of their adventure, along with moving them home for the summer—all contributed to the eye-opening reality that our relationship with them was changing fast. Our once-pretty-good relationship with our girls was deteriorating. Nobody wanted Dad's insights or advice anymore. And Mom was "helping" too much. How do we negotiate the uncertain waters of this phase of life?

As I often do, I sought encouragement at a local bookstore. *Surely someone has written about the trials and tribulations of parenting young adults,* I thought. Sadly, I found very little that was helpful. There are plenty of books written about parenting—but usually for the under-18 age-group, getting them through the troubled teen years, dealing with problem areas such as drugs, alcohol, or promiscuity.

If we had had any of those problems with our daughters,

I would have already scrambled for help. But we didn't. And believe me—we know we're fortunate. They were normal teenagers, bright, responsible, trustworthy, and basically good kids. We breathed a small sigh of pleasure when they graduated from high school, were accepted into college, and went off to their college campuses. And yet little hints started to pop up in our phone conversations or on their visits home that our usual parenting methods weren't working—we were being too protective, overly concerned, or not trusting enough.

What are we doing wrong? we wondered. *We're just being our normal parent selves, aren't we?* While we respected their new independence, we still wanted to be involved in their lives, to know their friends, to be aware of how their studies were going, and above all, to feel connected to them—in order to help them avoid the mistakes we made.

But it felt as if our girls were gently rebuffing our efforts. They didn't want us to be as involved as we once were. Other parents expressed similar concerns. Their budding adults seemed unappreciative and downright hostile at times. We all were asking ourselves, *What's the problem here? What can we do to maintain good communication and goodwill? What do other parents do to bridge this gap?*

I've learned that this is not a unique phenomenon. Many parents I've talked to have agreed that more needs to be said about parenting young adults. Because even though our culture has adopted the myth that our jobs are done once they've graduated from high school or college, nothing could be farther from the truth. The reality is, our role as parents continues well into adulthood. We'll always wear the title of "Mom" and "Dad." The key is to learn to understand and then navigate the uncertain waters of our role in our children's lives now that they're grown and on their way to independence. The parenting job is ever-changing—evolving, if you will—much as it did when you first brought your newborn home, to his or her stages as a toddler, then preschooler, and on up through his or her four years in high school. You had to adapt back then, and you have to adapt now.

We must move on to a new, higher level of parenting. Our jobs as parents are not yet complete—we must learn new communication skills. We must open our eyes to see our offspring as their own people, separate from us, and accordingly, we must fine-tune our antenna in our dealings with them.

This book covers what I've gleaned from my own experience and from other parents as well. At the heart of success is surrender to God and His will, plus practicing love in all its forms. We must learn to demonstrate it and apply it in different ways with each adult child. Sometimes love means restraint. Sometimes love means saying yes. Sometimes love means saying no. Sometimes love means being painfully honest. And sometimes love is saying nothing. Whatever the situation requires, we're still learning, still growing in the knowledge of God's love and how to appropriate it and pass it along to our kids.

At each encounter with my children, I've found it helpful to remind myself of my goal, which I've condensed into a simple question. It pops into my mind often these days, before I speak or do anything for my adult daughters. I ask myself, *Will this action or these words help build a healthier, stronger relationship with my child?* When I feel myself wanting to criticize or offer an opinion, I stop myself (most of the time) to wonder if my comments will promote what I'm aiming for in our relationship. More often than not, the answer is "Nope—that won't help."

My prayer is that as your parenting role develops, you'll abound in God's love. I pray that you'll see the need to surrender to Him in new ways while embracing the goal of promoting a new and better relationship with your children.

1

Relating Beyond Advice

There is . . . a time to be silent, and a time to speak (Eccles. 3:1, 7).

AL had always shared his knowledge with his children. In fact, he loved teaching them how to change the oil in the car, balance the checkbook, or ski down a "black diamond" mountain.

But Al was not prepared for his children to become adults. Within four years, all three of his children were out on their own. When they called, he asked questions, then proceeded to give them advice, just as he always had.

"Don't forget to get those tires checked now," he would say before hanging up.

Al's wife, Jenna, tried to talk to him about it.

"Honey, Annie told you that she could take care of the car while she's at college."

"Oh, I know—just giving her a friendly reminder," Al replied.

"She seemed, well, annoyed that you mentioned it to her again."

> Instructing and guiding your young adult children the way you did when they were younger is no longer needed or appreciated.

"She didn't seem that way to me," Al responded, oblivious to the signs.

A few months later, Al grumbled to Jenna: "When's the last time Brad called? I think I'll try to catch him." He entered the number.

"Hey, son! Glad I caught you. How's it going?"

Jenna listened, preparing herself.

"Just tell them . . . no, no—don't do it that way."

Turning away, Jenna groaned inwardly. *He's doing it again! After all the times I've suggested he back off with giving advice! He simply won't listen. He's pushing Brad and the girls away.*

A short time later, Al found Jenna in the kitchen and complained that Brad had brushed him off. "Said he had a study group. I wish he had time for a good talk."

Jenna recognized the problem, but Al refused to listen. And when their son tried to talk to him, Al didn't get it.

"Thanks, Dad, but I can deal with the bank myself."

"Oh, no problem, son. I'll just call Frank, and he can take care of it for me."

Al's insistence in helping only frustrated his son, who vowed to keep his problems to himself in the future.

Since his kids were little, Al has been giving them advice and guidance, like a good dad. The problem is, he still sees his children's problems as his problems—but they aren't. Now, as young adults, his children are growing toward complete independence, just as he taught them. Instructing and guiding them all the time as he did when they were younger is no longer needed or appreciated. Nor does it promote a healthy relationship with his kids. Recognizing that fact is the first step for Al. Backing off from advice, he needs to find a whole new way of connecting with his children, or he won't have much of a relationship with them in the future.

For other parents, the children are more direct. "Dad! Please!" Kelsie said, "I don't need you to always tell me how to do things. I know how to do it myself. You taught me—remember?"

Unfortunately, sometimes even the direct approach doesn't work. The end result? Exactly what we as parents don't want—we alienate our children. They withdraw, as Brad in the first story did.

From our side of the fence, it's frustrating to see our kids make the same mistakes we made. If only they would listen, they would save themselves so much hassle.

What is advice, really? That's easy, you say. Advice is to make recommendations, to counsel or teach. Some synonyms include *guidance, teaching, instruction, opinion, suggestion,* and *wisdom.* Giving advice is how parents have been nurturing since our children were born. It's second nature to teach, remind, and correct. It's how we show our loving concern.

The trouble is, adult children don't especially want to be guided, taught, or instructed by parents any longer. Not seeing our input as particularly loving, they respond with hostility or withdrawal.

Remember—they've already been shaped by years of our opinion-giving and suggestions. It's time they exercise their own wisdom muscles. So why don't we let them?

It's All About Control

At the heart of giving advice lies the issue of control. It's frightening to think of taking our hands off, to release our beloved child into the big, bad world. There's fear, the uncertainty of what might happen. But as parents with faith in Jesus Christ, we must surrender our desire to control and place our confidence and trust in God. We need to remind ourselves that He loves our children more than we do. He'll walk with them, wherever they go, whatever they're doing. Now our job as parents is to rest in that knowledge and surrender back to God the Father the control we've had since they were born.

Honest Confrontation

Karen's daughter-in-law opened her eyes to her need to change.

Michelle didn't mince words. "Karen," she said, "you're too controlling. You need to let us make our own decisions now."

Controlling. Me? Controlling? I thought I was only being caring. Instead of taking offense at Michelle's words, Karen spent time thinking about them. She finally concluded that Michelle was right. After all, hadn't she (Karen) worried that her son's recently purchased car might not be good on mileage? And hadn't she taken it upon herself to hunt all over town for the best deal on house paint for them? And hadn't she worried that he might be renewing friendships with some old buddies who had once been a bad influence on him?

Back off. Back off . . . were the words that began to come to Karen each time she found herself running his life. And the best thing is, two pluses came out of her daughter-in-law's candor: (1) the great relief at knowing she (Karen) didn't have to figure out everything about her children's lives as well as her own, (2) the realization that just as she was controlling her kids' lives, she tended to be a controlling person in other areas also—with her husband and friends.

"I'm thankful that instead of hiding frustrations and resentments, my daughter-in-law had the boldness to speak up. And I'm thankful I listened."

Heeding Our Spouses

"My husband tried to tell me I was giving too much advice to our grown son and his wife on everything from buying a car to whether or not their toddler was big enough to handle grapes," Marilyn said.

"A sample conversation might go like this: 'Let them be,' Paul would say. 'They need to make their own decisions.'

"'But what if it's the wrong one? What if they go buy that house and it's more than they can afford? What if they haven't even thought about property taxes?'

"'Then they'll find out. But it has to be their experience—not ours,' Paul said.

"'Then what can we do?'

"'We can be available for discussion. Pray about it. And that's it.'

"'I can't. I can't just do nothing when I know more about what they're doing than they do.'

"'Marilyn,' my husband said, sighing, 'instead of appreciating your wonderful advice, you'll only make enemies. Let them be!'

"It took a few more bouts of offering my son and daughter-in-law unwanted advice, but guess what? The more I held

> Ask yourself this question: Will this action or these words help me build a healthier, stronger relationship with my child?

my tongue, the more the two of them began asking for my advice!"

Author Mary Deatrick in her book *It Hurts to Love*, relates this visual exercise to help release our children to God:

> Picture in your mind putting your son or daughter in a gift box. Then wrap the box with beautiful party paper and ribbon. Then imagine the glorious throne of God situated at the top of a flight of stairs. In your mind, walk up those stairs with your gift-wrapped package and put it down at the feet of Jesus, who sits on the throne. Wait as Jesus bends, picks up the package, puts it on His lap, removes the wrappings, takes off the box lid and lifts your child out. After you have seen Jesus holding your child, then walk back down the stairs, turning midway to look back and assure yourself that Jesus is still holding your youngster. Thank God for taking control.[1]

In our desire to connect with our children on an adult, mature level, we must keep asking ourselves the question *Will this action or these words help in my goal to build a healthier, stronger relationship with my child?* By trusting, accepting, respecting, withholding our advice, and relinquishing control, we're sending a powerful message of affirmation. It's like saying, "I know you can do it." Saying nothing is nonverbal communication that speaks more powerfully than any amount of words.

Simply Listen

Carrie's 22-year-old daughter, Amber, shared an apartment in another part of the state. She called home to say she was having a bad week and wanted to come for a weekend visit.

Carrie said, "Did you lose your job?"

"No," Amber said.

"Did you have a disagreement with your boyfriend?"

"No," Amber replied.

She arrived Friday evening and spent some time with a hometown friend before coming home. That night her dad sat with her outside as they did some stargazing and talking. When he came in, he told Carrie that their daughter was fine, just discouraged about the demands of the real world. Along with rent and bills, her student loans and car insurance were coming due soon.

Carrie listened to her daughter too. Her complaints were nothing major—just life issues all adults have to deal with.

"So," Carrie says, "we did what we could do. We listened and encouraged. There was nothing we could do to solve anything, and even if there was, she didn't want it solved. She just wanted some tender loving care from her mom and dad."

Fortunately, Carrie and her husband recognized their daughter's need to simply "be" without offering advice or, worse, trying to fix her problems.

A Kinder, Gentler Guidance

"I try really hard not to toss out my two cents' worth all the time. Maybe it's still in the realm of advice-giving, but what works for me is to share stories from my own life. I'm not preachy or anything. I just tell it like it happened and don't offer any kind of moral. I just let it be. Somehow, it's softer, and my daughters seem to respond better."

"Sometimes," Jim says, "the best thing to do is tell the kids where they can go to get the help they need instead of my always having to be the problem-solver or the advice-giver. I'll give them the name and number of a financial adviser I know and leave it at that. It's their choice as to whether they call him or not. In the past, I would have been all over them, telling them how to invest their money and fund their IRAs. I still bite my tongue a lot, but I think our communication has improved."

Waiting Until Asked

Harvey's son, Paul, was considering moving his wife and young family to be closer to his roots in a remote part of Montana, near his parents. Paul and Jan were fed up with city life and wanted a nice, small town in which to raise their family.

"What do you think, Dad?" they asked.

Harvey says his kids expect him to have an answer for everything. "*The buck stops here* is what they think. Only problem is, I didn't have a clue as to what would be best for them. Of course, we want our son and his family nearby, but I doubted they would be able to get jobs in their field so far from the city. So I suggested they make a list with two columns, one for the pluses and one for the minuses. At the end of a certain period of time, say two weeks, put all the facts together and make a decision. And make sure it's unanimous."

"Thanks, Dad," Paul said. "You always know what to do."

Harvey admits he was dumbfounded. "I do? I thought I was passing the buck. All I did was share a little wisdom." There are adult children, too, who are so dependent on their parents' wisdom that they can't seem to make a move without calling home. While parents might secretly love the frequent consultations, being a crutch for our children doesn't help them become separate, independent people. They constantly call and want to know what to do or how to tackle a problem. Wise parents recognize that providing the answers for their maturing children is not helping them develop their own decision-making skills. Easing out of the advice-giving role, in this instance, may be the path of least resistance and the course of best, wisest wisdom.

Helping Them Develop Decision-Making Skills

When Marlene called home about a new job opportunity, she laid out the benefits of the new position as well as the present job, expecting her parents to tell her which way to go.

Instead, Frank and Maggie asked questions:

- "Would this be a step up for you?"
- "Would you be challenged by the new duties?"
- "Will it give you more responsibility?"
- "Will you be happy?"
- "Is the pay raise significant?"
- "Will you be required to work longer hours?"

By asking the right questions, you help your children express the concerns and challenges of the decision. Pray with them about it, on the phone and in your own devotional time, asking for God's wisdom for them as they make the choice.

Frank and Maggie determined that their daughter would not be as happy in the new position, but they didn't tell her that. They let her work through it, and eventually she came to the same conclusion, maturing in the process.

Maggie said, "Honey, Dad and I think you made the right decision. We're proud of you."

As easy as it would have been for them to tell their daughter what they thought and why, they recognized that the lesson of learning to make important life decisions is far more crucial to master.

A Biblical Example: The Prodigal Son

The Bible offers parents all kinds of wisdom, even with adult children. In the story of the prodigal son, we see an example of a parent who did not offer unsolicited advice. He's the perfect role model for this stage of parenting. (See Luke 15:11-32.)

When his son came to him and asked for his inheritance, the father could have said, "No way," or he could have given it to his son with all kinds of advice and strings attached. Of course, he had to have known that this son might squander his share of the family wealth, leaving him penniless for his future. And it had to have been excruciating to hold his tongue, not to offer advice or strings. Why didn't he?

In this father's wisdom, he knew the lessons his son would learn would be far greater than the loss of an inheritance (although in our materialistic culture especially, this is very hard to accept).

So what did the son gain by his father's lack of advice-giving? First, he learned humility. After wasting his fortune on foolish pleasures, he was left to feed on the slop of pigs.

It was in that time of humiliation and need that he realized that his father's servants were treated far better than he was. In the shadow of his own immaturity and selfishness, he saw his parent in a new light—the light of respect, the light of generosity and goodness.

SOME ADULT CHILDREN ARE SO DEPENDENT ON MOM AND DAD THAT THEY CAN'T MAKE A MOVE WITHOUT CALLING HOME.

So the son returned home, humbled, destitute, with all trace of boastfulness gone. His father welcomed him back with open arms, happy to see his son again. How could he do that, this wise father? Didn't he want to scream and shout at his child for all his selfish waste? My guess is that he did, but he must have realized it would serve no useful purpose in his son's maturation process. No words were needed. He must have remembered the goal—to maintain a relationship with his adult child.

This biblical father trusted completely in God's ability to watch over his son. He didn't exert his own manipulations to control his son, to try and shape him into the man he wanted him to become. Instead, he surrendered to God's sovereignty to complete the process his son was in. He trusted God with the results. It's time for us to do the same.

Up until now, our parenting task has been to teach our children to make wise decisions, to become independent people. By the time they enter adulthood, they're ready to test their wings and prove they can make it on their own and be ready to teach their own children.

Our comfort is that God's Word abounds with wisdom, and through prayer and listening we receive the guidance we need. God speaks to us, but ultimately we have free will to make decisions about our lives. We should follow God's parenting example and allow our adult children the same privilege to choose their own way.

Parenting Pointers

In learning to live beyond giving advice, you can take the following steps:

1. Listen for cues from your children that you're offering too much.
   - Are they annoyed when you offer advice?
   - Are they avoiding you?
   - Are you constantly reminding them, asking them questions?
   - Are you ignoring their requests to back off?
   - Are you honoring their ability to manage?
   - Have they asked you openly to stop giving advice?
2. Surrender your children to God.
   - Do you trust God?
   - Do you believe God is capable of caring for your children?
   - Are you practicing what you believe—that is, it is important to release your children by stepping back?
3. Ask yourself, *Will this action or these words help to build a healthier, stronger relationship with my children?*
   - Do I accept my children?
   - Do I respect my children?
   - Do I acknowledge my children as adults now?

- Do I try to control my adult children?
- Do I believe that withholding advice will send a powerful, affirming message to my children?
- Do I help my children to problem-solve for themselves?
- Do I point them to where they can get the advice they need from others?

2

Facing Disappointment

Trust in the L*ORD* *with all your heart and lean not on your own understanding* (Prov. 3:5).

HELENE and Jim's 25-year-old son, Mark, was independent and impulsive, almost from birth. Life excited him; he feared little. Out on his own, living in another city, early one Saturday morning he called his parents. He usually didn't call so early, and Helene's heart skipped a beat as she wondered if everything was okay.

"Mom! Dad! Guess what! I've met the perfect girl. Her name is Marcy. She's everything I'm looking for. We're getting married!"

"What? Married? But we haven't even met her!"

This was the first Helene and Jim had heard of the girl. Helene did her best to keep her emotions in check.

"Mark, you can't get married—how long have you known this girl?"

"A couple of months. She's wonderful, Mom. I'm crazy about her!"

"We're glad you've found someone you care about, son,

but please wait! Don't rush into this. Get to know her better first—let your family meet her."

"I love her, Mom. She wants to get married as soon as possible. It's romantic. No point in waiting. We know we love each other."

Helene and Jim tried calling their son back, but they ended up playing phone tag most of the week without ever connecting.

The following Saturday the phone rang again. Helene and Jim got a call that stopped them cold.

Mark's voice, while excited, was guarded and a bit distant. "We did it! I'm a married man!"

Helene handed the phone to her husband, tears spilling down her cheeks. How could her son do such a thing? They hadn't even met the girl!

Needless to say, Helene and Jim were disappointed, hurt, and worried about why their son would rush into a marriage this way. *Hadn't we talked many times about the importance of taking your time, learning all you can about your intended? It's a lifetime decision!*

In spite of their deeply wounded feelings, they sent a large bouquet of congratulatory flowers—the biggest their budget would allow. It carried with it a simple note: "Congratulations and best wishes! Love, Mom and Dad."

In time, they learned the truth about "wonderful Marcy." At 35, she was an experienced manipulator. She had been married before and seemed to know how to play on a gullible young man. They learned she had pushed hard for the elopement in an effort to isolate him from his family and friends. Mark, lonely and naive, had been easy prey.

From experience, Helene and Jim knew Marcy wasn't genuine in her love for their son. They could have rushed in to try to save him from the inevitable, but they knew Mark wouldn't listen. He was young, infatuated, blinded by his emotions. Helene and Jim prayed and waited.

Within a couple of months, Mark knew that he wasn't in paradise anymore. His head whirled with confusion. When he met Marcy, he had a two-bedroom, fully-furnished apartment and two automobiles. By the time he came to his senses, he had nothing left of material worth.

Helene and Jim suffered along with their son, agonized for him, prayed daily for him, and eagerly awaited his calls and visits. In the meantime, they disciplined themselves to "let go and let God" by withholding advice and opinions. They felt Mark needed to find his own way out of this situation.

Marcy used every trick she knew to keep Mark on the hook. For a while it worked. Slowly Mark began to recognize the truth about his marriage, how destructive and codependent it was.

Inevitably, *the* call came.

"It's over," Mark announced to his parents, defeat heavy in his voice.

Helene and Jim recognized their opportunity. Mark was broken, willing to listen, asking for their wisdom.

Mark freed himself by moving away, divorcing Marcy, and by refusing to be drawn into any more of her emotional pleas. Later they learned that Marcy had been married several times before and had several emotional problems.

Helene and Jim offered their love at every opportunity to help Mark navigate through the grief and disillusionment. But what about *their* disappointment? Is it so wrong to have hopes and dreams for their son, that he find the right woman to marry and share life with? Disappointment and disillusionment occur when our deepest expectations aren't met. Either what we hope for our children doesn't happen, or what we dread comes to pass. What exactly is an expectation? It's an anticipation, an expectancy, an awaiting, a presumption, a calculation, an anticipatory desire, a hope, an assurance, a trust, a reliance, a dependence, a likelihood.

DISAPPOINTMENT AND DISILLUSIONMENT OCCUR WHEN OUR DEEPEST EXPECTATIONS AREN'T MET.

When unmet expectations are high, parents can experience a knee-jerk response about their parenting ability. "Where have we gone wrong?" we ask. "What could we have done differently?"

While we can't blame ourselves for our children's actions, in truth, such disappointments can be a catalyst for change. If we look within ourselves, we may discover that we've been holding on to secret expectations. Uncovering those presumptions is the first step toward change.

It's not wrong to have hopes and dreams for our children, of course. But to expect them to happen the way *we* want isn't based on reality. Our expectations are simply *our* wishes. Put another way, harboring expectations is another, albeit subtle, form of control.

Pride and Expectations Revealed

Ethel experienced extreme disappointment with her daughter when she announced her divorce.

"I remember being in the shower, crying buckets and

buckets. Finally, it occurred to me that I was overly upset about this. I had to sit down and ask myself why I was so worked up. In the end," she said, blushing with embarrassment, "it was about *my* pride that no one in our family had ever divorced. It was humiliating to me that *my* child was the first.

"I think whenever a parent responds the way I did, in an overly emotional way, it's time for self-examination. There may be a core issue at the heart of it all that needs to be rooted out once and for all."

Author Anne Lamott says in her novel *Crooked Little Heart*, "Expectations are resentments waiting to happen."[1] By allowing expectations to live and grow in our minds, we're playing with fire. Ultimately, they threaten all our relationships, but especially those with our children. It's important to explore our thought life, to see if we presume the path our child's life will take. If so, those presumptions need to be dissected completely in the light of day.

- Where do they come from?
- Do they stem from your life's experiences? Your childhood? Your failings? Your aspirations? Your family's hopes for *you*?
- How do they affect you as a parent?
- Are pride and control at the root of it?
- Is your expectation a true reflection of you as a parent, the job you've done?

Maybe you're disappointed that your son chose not to go to college. Maybe he prefers a trade or wants to become a musician or a sculptor. Maybe you learned your son or daughter is involved in a sexual relationship. Maybe he or she is choosing a homosexual lifestyle, and you worry about health issues. Maybe you don't like your daughter's choice of a mate. He's not what you consider to be "good enough" for your little girl. Maybe your child doesn't opt to live the way you do. Maybe less is more for him, and you don't understand that.

What if our disappointment isn't over our child's choices but with his or her circumstances?

Helen's daughter Justine had settled herself into a successful career in a city a few states away from her parents when she started experiencing bouts of depression. Over time, the depression deepened, even with medication. Helen confided to me that she feared her daughter's problem was far worse than clinical depression; she feared mental illness. This mother's sad weariness and disappointment were based not on a choice but on life's circumstances. Even so, at the heart of her disappointment were expectations—that her daughter would have a good and fulfilling life, a happy life.

Her disappointment is sharp. It's no one's fault. Her hopes for her daughter's life may not come to pass. How will she deal with her disappointment?

Looking more deeply into ourselves, we're confronted with the question of where our hope is anchored and what we actually need to survive and continue. Disappointment is meant to be a divine checkpoint on our journey of faith. We must declare to ourselves and to God *where* we're seeking our sufficiency.

Jeremiah 29:11 records, "'I know the plans I have for you,' declares the LORD, 'plans to prosper you and not to harm you, plans to give you hope and a future.'"

God has a unique plan for each of us, our children included. We must take our disappointments and expectations and give them to God so we aren't blocking His work in our child's life. Then we must believe, trusting in *His* ability to bring it to fruition.

In light of that, we understand how futile it is to hope our child will go *our* prescribed way—living out *our* expectations. As we accept the fact that God has a plan for each of us, the day will come when we'll answer to Him alone for the path we've chosen. Is it our job to determine our child's way in life? Or His?

> IT ISN'T REALISTIC TO EXPECT OUR HOPES AND DREAMS FOR OUR CHILDREN TO PLAY OUT JUST THE WAY WE WANT.

If we acknowledge that our expectations may be in direct conflict with God's ultimate plan for our children, then, of course, we must surrender those expectations to the Lord. What do we *do* with our feelings of disappointment or deep sadness? Recognize them for what they are—feelings—then take them captive to the obedience of Christ.

"We demolish arguments and every pretension that sets itself up against the knowledge of God, and we take captive every thought to make it obedient to Christ" (2 Cor. 10:5).

I've learned it's okay to openly express my feelings to the Lord, telling Him frankly how I feel. Then I simply say, *Lord, as a sacrifice of obedience and love to you, I'm giving you this disappointment or sadness. I trust in your divine plan for my child.*

When we release our feelings and expectations to God, we free ourselves to be true vessels of love toward our child. When we're bound up by our emotions and expectations, we're restricting our capacity to be effective as Christians, as people, as parents.

Letting go of our children does not only mean physically but also releasing them within our hearts. How can we know if we've truly let go? When pride is no longer involved, when we no longer ask ourselves, *How could she do this to me?* or *What will people think?* When we stop thinking of ourselves as the victims, then we know our hands have released them.

Acceptance of the Will of God

Cliff Barrows, long-time music and program director for the Billy Graham Evangelistic Association, in an article in *Decision* magazine tells about a conversation with his father shortly before his death:

> Dad couldn't see, and he could hardly hear; nor did he recognize my voice. I was the only one in the room that day, and I decided: I'm going to ask Dad some questions about Cliff.

Without his dad recognizing his voice, Cliff asked, "What did you and Mrs. Barrows want Cliff to become?"

> Without hesitation, he reminisced, "We wanted him to become a surgeon. We thought he would make a good doctor."
>
> I knew that this was true because the notion was ingrained into me. I wrote term papers about doctors and medicine.
>
> I was set for that direction, I thought—until God spoke to my heart.
>
> Turning to Dad again, I asked, "Did Cliff become a surgeon?"
>
> He shook his head. "No . . . he became a song leader for Billy Graham, and he preaches once in a while."

Then I asked, "Mr. Barrows, were you disappointed? Your aspiration was for Cliff to become a surgeon."

Dad waited quite a few seconds and then turned in my direction. With a little smile, he said, "No. He had to do the will of God."

I put my arms around him. "Dad," I said, "this is Cliff speaking to you."

He laughed. "You rascal! You tricked me!"

As I hugged him, I said, "I will always be proud to tell people about my father. You've set an example for me that I am passing on."[2]

Mr. Barrows might have been disappointed initially about his son's path, but he recognized *his* desires were not God's desires. He's a good role model for all of us.

A common mistake we parents make is to assume that because we raised our child with our values and morals, our child will embrace our ideas as his or her own. We see our son or daughter, on some level, perhaps unconsciously, as simply smaller versions of ourselves. But the reality is that your child is most likely very different from you.

Honest respect for another person involves, at least partially, an understanding of personality differences. That holds true with our soon-to-be-grown children. We need to understand the way they think and process communication. Doing this will avoid many misunderstandings and may avert our disappointment to some extent.

Florence Littauer, the originator of CLASS (Christian Leaders Authors Speakers Seminar), in her book *Personality Plus*[3] breaks the personalities into the four well-known groups: the sanguine, the choleric, the phlegmatic, and the melancholy.

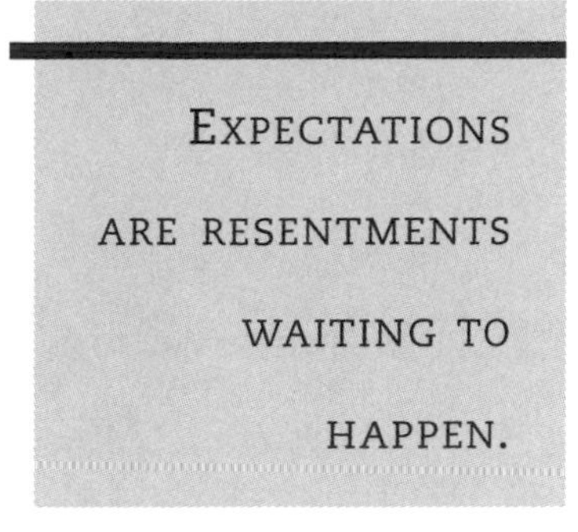

The sanguine personality is described best by the word *fun*. Sanguines are the popular life of the party, focused on making fun out of life in every way possible. They are turbo-charged, outgoing, optimistic, and are energized by being around other people. Conversely, they need to learn to stay on track, to tone down their fun. They're weak on organization.

Cholerics are the *powerful* personality type. They're self-assured, natural leaders, ambitious, very focused, and have natural stage presence. On the other hand, they tend to be impatient with people, demanding, and seemingly unfriendly. They need to lighten up and develop warmth. They're energized by people.

The phlegmatic's best descriptive word is *peaceful*. Even-keeled, attentive, and good listeners—often called the "chameleon" personality, because they can be excellent leaders when they want—phlegmatics prefer to stay in the background. They rise to the occasion. Alternatively, they can lean toward laziness and procrastination. They derive energy from solitude.

The melancholy personality strives for *perfection*. Sensitive and caring, they prefer to remain on a schedule and focus well on details. This personality tends to be artistic and introverted. They're drained by people, tend to be pessimistic, and are energized by solitude.

When we understand the personality differences of our adult children, we're better able to extend grace to them. Grasping the fact that our sanguine, life-of-the-party daugh-

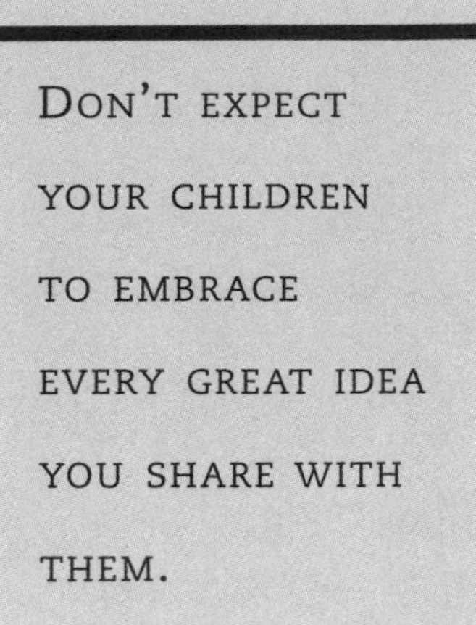

ter isn't interested at all in joining the family's law firm or that our melancholy, artistic son doesn't want to become a professional football player certainly helps in short-circuiting our expectations, subsequent disappointment, and the strife and turmoil that may ensue.

A Biblical Example: Adam and Eve

Genesis 3 describes the temptation and fall of Adam and Eve. God told them the one thing they couldn't do was eat the fruit from the tree in the middle of the garden. We all know the story. Of course, they did just that.

How disappointed God the Father must have been! He couldn't even count on His children to do the one thing He asked.

What was His response? He laid out the consequences first to Eve, then Adam. They were cast out of the garden forever and suffered because of it. And yet, throughout history, Father God is making provisions to overcome His disappointment with humanity by sending His only Son to come to earth to become our Redeemer. Jesus bridges the gap that sin and rebellion have created. His ultimate goal with us, His children, is reconciliation. He wants to have a relationship with us. His example should inspire us as we deal with the disappointments our own children bring to us. Our goal is a worthy one: to promote and nurture a healthy relationship with our adult children.

Parenting Pointers

When facing disappointment with your adult child, you can take the following steps:

1. Explore your thought life.
   - Are you trying to exert control over your children?
   - Do you harbor unrealistic expectations?
   - Are you able to let go of your expectations once you become aware of them?
   - Do you believe God has a divine plan for not only you but also your children?
   - Can you acknowledge that perhaps your desires for your children may be in direct conflict with God's plan?
   - Have you taken into account your adult children's personality types as part of trying to understand them?
2. Recognize your disappointment as valid feelings.
   - Express your disappointment to the Lord the way the psalmist David did so often.
   - Vent your emotions to God in prayer.
   - Be obedient to take your thoughts captive to the obedience of Christ, surrendering them to God once and for all.
   - Recommit. Your hope is in Christ alone, not in *your* plan.
3. Remember your goal and keep asking yourself, *Will this action or these words help build a healthier, stronger relationship with my adult child?*

3

Surviving Their Bad Decisions

All have sinned and fall short of the glory of God (Rom 3:23).

Prayerful Intervention

Jim and Betsy's daughter Carrie married on the rebound after the painful break-up of her long engagement. She started dating a fellow she knew from church who had been admiring her for a long time. A few months later, she told her parents she was pregnant and wanted to marry Steve. They agreed.

After a difficult pregnancy with many health problems, a son was born, and the young couple seemed to be settling into married life. Within the year, though, Carrie was pregnant again. This pregnancy was even more difficult, combining health issues along with a baby to care for. After their daughter was born, Steve lost his job, and the couple fell on hard times. In time, he found another position, but it took them a while to get out of the debt they got into while he was unemployed.

Again, Carrie found herself pregnant. It was the worst pregnancy of the three, with hospitalizations and frequent doctor visits. With two toddlers already, she found the stress was great. It was about this time that Betsy and Jim couldn't ignore certain things about Steve. He would come home with big-ticket items he had just purchased, like a home entertainment unit, even though they had many outstanding bills.

This pattern persisted for many months. Bill collectors called regularly. Carrie complained to Steve, but he always said he would take care of it. Carrie believed him—but he did *not* take care of it.

God can use your child's failures to remake the inner person in ways that would be impossible if he or she always succeeded.

When the washer broke down, there was no money to repair or replace it. Betsy and Jim agonized over what to do for their grown daughter. They had helped financially in the past, but they couldn't keep bailing out the young couple, couldn't keep paying their heating bill or the phone bill. They felt by repairing the washer they would not only be enabling Steve's poor behavior but would also be providing an all-too-comfortable safety net for their daughter. At the same time, they saw the hard spot their daughter was in. With three small children, diapers, and piles of laundry every day, she couldn't live without a washing machine for long.

They decided that Betsy would go over after work twice a

week and bring the clothes home to launder. Their daughter and grandchildren would have clean clothes, but they would not encourage Steve's terrible behavior. They hoped that guilt and a sense of responsibility for his young family would spur him into making correct choices.

In time, Betsy was the one who suffered. Trying to work full time and do loads and loads of extra laundry plus the time transporting the clothes back and forth in the winter was wearing her down.

Finally, it became clear that Steve's problems weren't just poor judgment. They discovered he was a drug user—always had been. He had successfully hidden it from everyone, even his young wife, and was spending the bulk of his paycheck on his habit.

Betsy and Jim prayed long and hard about their decision to intervene for their daughter and grandchildren. They moved their daughter and grandchildren in with them, forcing Steve to take action, to get himself into rehabilitation.

For a while it seemed to be working. The young couple reconciled. During that time, Carrie became pregnant with a fourth child. Soon, though, it became apparent that Steve had no intention of turning his life around.

In this instance, after much prayer again, stepping in to rescue their daughter and four grandchildren was the right thing to do for Betsy and Jim. Carrie had four children to consider. She needed a job, and they all needed health care and a place to live. Her parents felt it was their responsibility before God to help provide an avenue to help her get her life back in order.

They built an addition to their house for the large family they've acquired. After Carrie recuperates from her recent

C-section, she'll start training for a new job. Childcare is one of the benefits of this new position.

Sometimes our children's problems are self-induced, and sometimes they're simply life's circumstances. This incident with Carrie seems to be some of both. While they knew they couldn't "fix" the situation their daughter found herself in, Betsy and Jim are helping her pick up the pieces to construct a new life.

Failure means a lack of success, a falling short. The word spells *judgment*, usually self-imposed. Personal failure brings even the toughest of us to our knees. Yet failure can be one of God's most powerful tools for remaking the inner person in ways that would otherwise have been impossible. Failure makes us humble, real, and relatable to others—something success can't do. Potential will develop as we seek to understand failure and use it to our advantage. Paul says in 2 Cor. 12:9, "I am glad to boast about how weak I am; I am glad to be a living demonstration of Christ's power" (TLB).

Offering a Way of Escape

Al and Bettie's daughter Martina had been married a few years. She and her husband were seeking to buy a house in southern California, where prices were high. They found a house in a good part of town and entered into a lease-option agreement. They put $4,000 down and moved into the house, paying higher than normal rent, with the agreement that at the end of one year, if they decided to buy the house, all monies would go toward the purchase price.

Over a few months' time, in dealings with their landlord, both Martina and her husband started experiencing doubts about the wisdom of the decision they had made. They wanted to get into the market so badly that they pushed their doubts aside. Besides, they didn't want to lose their $4,000 investment.

When Martina's parents came for a visit and heard the details of the arrangement, they were troubled. After talking it over and praying about it, they made an offer to Martina and her husband. They considered the goal of how to promote a healthier, stronger relationship with their adult children and presented their offer accordingly.

REMEMBER: NOT EVEN THE BEST UPBRINGING AND PERFECT HOME ENVIRONMENT GUARANTEES THE RESULTS YOU HOPE FOR.

"We would like to give you $4,000 with the understanding that you'll walk away from this agreement at the end of the lease," Al and Bettie said gently.

"We can't accept that from you," their son-in-law said.

"Oh, it's not a gift," Al said. "It's an investment we want to make in the house you finally do buy."

After praying about it and discussing their options, Martina and her husband decided to accept the money. They had never taken money from her parents before, but because of the way Al and Bettie presented it, they felt they could. The young couple experienced great relief when all was said and done. They hadn't realized how much the situation had stressed them. But in their wisdom and long years of living, Martina's parents recognized the bad situation—one where their loved ones would be over-extended and ultimately their relationship taxed. To them the $4,000 was a small gift to an otherwise self-sufficient couple.

Severing Ties

One poignant example of not intervening comes from the family of former United States Senator George McGovern, who followed the advice of experts to cut off communication with his 33-year-old daughter, Terri, an alcoholic and a drug addict. Her therapists believed it best for McGovern and his wife not to contact Terri so she would take responsibility for her addiction and bad decisions. It was during this period of no contact that Terri died after falling into the snow in a drunken stupor. In his response to this tragedy, McGovern wrote a book, *Terri*, in which he admonishes parents to stay close to their grown children, especially when they're in trouble. McGovern's experience presents an extreme case, but it's a cautionary tale for people considering the hard-line approach of completely severing family ties in response to their children's bad decisions.[1]

Parenting the Grandkids

Across the United States, nearly 2.5 million grandparents currently are raising more than 4.5 million grandchildren, according to the 2000 census. Estimates are that the number of children living in grandparent-headed households has risen 30 percent since 1990.[2]

Many reasons such as teen pregnancy, poverty, drug abuse, death, imprisonment, and mental illness are responsible for the record number of parents unable to care for their children. And yet grandparents help keep the family together, providing continuity and familiarity for the grandchild in a very difficult situation.

The bond between grandparent and grandchild is intensified by the relationship both have with the missing parent, particularly when he or she is still alive. Some may be required to testify against their children in court in order to win custody of the grandchildren, while others live in fear that the parent will take the child back before he or she is ready.

An often-expressed regret is missing out on being grandparents—the feeling of "This isn't what I planned." That sense of loss is especially painful when one's own child has failed as a parent.

When self-blame enters our thinking, we need to remember that not even the best upbringing and perfect home environment guarantee the results we want.

Assigning Blame

Author Barbara Johnson is a mother well acquainted with feelings of failure and grief. Two of her sons died young, one in Vietnam, the other killed by a drunk driver. When her third son announced he was gay and disappeared into a lifestyle that was personally repugnant to her, she fell apart. Barbara has experienced much emotional healing and has seen her third son restored to a healthy lifestyle and walk with the Lord. She has this to say about undue guilt: "Parents are always asking, 'Where did I go wrong?' I tell them that God was a perfect parent, and look at the big mess He had with Adam! Who are we to think that we can be parents and not have big problems with our kids?"[3]

In other words, we should expect disappointment rather

than be surprised by it. Disappointment and failure are part of the human condition. As parents, perhaps we should shift our focus and recognize these times as opportunities for connection and greater influence. It would be easy to throw up our hands and disappear from our adult children's lives. But how would such an action promote our goal of a healthier, stronger relationship with our adult children? Often they need the sense of being loved more than they know.

Not to Blame—but Paying the Price Anyway

In his book *Once a Parent, Always a Parent*, Stephen A. Bly tells this story:

> Geoffrey and Marcia were selected by their city as Citizens of the Year in 1988. From his position as manager of the bank and hers as kindergarten teacher, they had, in their 20-plus years in the community, touched the lives of almost every family. Just the mention of their names brought a sense of honesty, stability, and credibility to any conversation.
>
> That's why it came as a shock when the newspapers blared the story of how their son, Allen, had been arrested for embezzling $32,000 from the new car dealership where he was the accountant.
>
> Rumors were circulated that it must have been difficult for him to grow up in a home with such perfect parents. Some people began to wonder aloud if the pressure to perform had been too great. Even Geoff and Marcia struggled to find fault in themselves.
>
> But Allen's problem was all his own. During college he began a secret habit of gambling—poker in the dorms, bets on sporting events, an occasional trip to the casinos. As

DISAPPOINTMENT AND FAILURE ARE PART OF THE HUMAN CONDITION.

his income grew, so did his addiction, until he began losing more than he made. He began skimming a little at work. Finally, he was caught. It should have been no more surprising than if it had happened to the son of the town drunk. Behavior does not necessarily reflect home environment.[4]

Allen chose a string of very bad decisions, all of which he'll pay the consequences for. Undoubtedly, his parents will pay as well. Loss of reputation, and perhaps even business, may be the result for them. While Geoff and Marcia will suffer because of their son's actions, they're not responsible. As an adult with free will, Allen alone is obligated to answer for the wrongs he committed.

The first step toward healing is to forgive. We demonstrate our forgiveness and acceptance of our adult children by not bringing up the matter repeatedly, by not discussing it with other people. We don't sit around letting the situation gnaw away at us.

As followers of Jesus Christ, we have no right to condemn our children—ever. The Bible says, "All have sinned and fall short of the glory of God" (Rom. 3:23). Remember the words of Jesus when the crowds were ready to stone the woman who was caught in the act of adultery: "If any one of you is without sin, let him be the first to throw a stone at her" (John 8:7). The message is that we're to love all who stray, including our children, just as God loves us. We'll have our greatest influence if we accept our children, spend time with them, communicate with them, and demonstrate our love for them, even though we don't approve of their choices or lifestyle.

As parents who are left with the fallout of our children's bad decisions, how do we move on after we've forgiven them? We can offer noncondemning statements that we hope will create a climate in which our adult children can receive and even request our advice. It's crucial that we recognize their autonomy and give them freedom to continue to make their own choices, just as our Heavenly Father does with us.

LET YOUR ADULT CHILDREN KNOW YOU LOVE THEM EVEN WHEN YOU DON'T APPROVE OF THEIR CHOICES.

They may well suffer the consequences of those choices. If they do begin to reap negative consequences from what we believe are poor decisions in their sexual behavior, we dare not limit or actively remove those consequences of their behavior. We can walk with them through those painful consequences. That's part of being supportive. It's in this context that many parents build deep and abiding relationships with their broken and suffering young adults. Our emotional support may be exactly what they need to help them make the necessary corrections in this part of life.

In picking up the pieces and surviving our children's bad decisions, we parents often do suffer. As we've seen from the examples cited here and from our own experiences, parents as well as children can live with consequences, whether it's a tainted reputation, raising the grandchildren, or worst of all, losing a child by death. Our focus must be on God's plan and provision and on our ability to surrender to His divine plan. When we lose sight of that focus, we can find ourselves mired in misery and depression. Seeking solace in God's strength and wisdom is what enables us to continue in our role as parents to our adult children.

A Biblical Example: Samson

Samson is a character in the Bible well known for his strength. God set him apart for a special mission: to begin to deliver the Israelites from the Philistines. His hair was his secret weapon. If cut, he would lose his strength. Samson's downfall was Delilah, a woman who was not a Jew. She nagged him every day to expose the secret of his strength. Finally he relented, and Delilah betrayed him. Samson was captured and his eyes put out. His actions can certainly be classified as a bad decision.

Yet in the last part of chapter 16 of Judges, we read that Samson turned back to God and prayed one last time, "O Sovereign LORD, remember me. O God, please strengthen me just once more" (v. 28). God heard his prayer and redeemed his bad decision by allowing him to destroy the Philistines, thereby completing his purpose on earth.

Parenting Pointers

In learning to pick up the pieces, in order to survive the bad decisions your children make, you can take the following steps:

1. Provide some assistance, framed in a respectful way.
   - Consider their independence.

- Consider their personality type.
- Consider their history.
- Consider their thinking on the subject, their motivations. Honor them.

2. Provide intervention if a crisis situation occurs.
   - Is it an emergency?
   - Have they exhausted their resources?
   - Are they capable of handling it themselves?
   - Are they healthy enough to deal with the situation?
   - Forgive them.
   - Look for opportunities to grow from the experience.
   - Stay involved by offering unconditional love and support.

3. Don't blame yourself.

4. Keep surrendering to God's plan.

Remember the goal, and ask yourself, *Will this action or these words help to build a healthier, stronger relationship with my adult child?*

4

Saying No and Giving Less

Discretion will protect you,
and understanding will guard you (Prov. 2:11).

TED was born the oldest in a family of four boys, and he excelled at everything he tried. He was Ralph and Margaret's pride and joy. They nurtured him, encouraged him to become a doctor, and sacrificed to put him through one of the country's top medical schools.

Ted graduated with honors and married, and Ralph and Margaret willingly cosigned numerous loans to help him establish himself in a practice. After a year or two, telltale signs started to pop up that things weren't going well. Creditors started calling. Patients complained. All he needed was another loan to carry him over. Soon other family members were asked to help bail him out. Everyone, of course, rallied around the star of the family.

Marital infidelities, white-collar drug use, and loan sharks were huge red flags to many family members. "Enough," they said. "No more loans. We're not helping the situation."

But Ted's parents proudly stated, "We believed in him when others didn't." They never recognized the need to change their tactics in helping their son become successful. Instead, they continued to coddle him, giving him more money each time he asked, enabling him in his lifestyle and his continuing decline. Clearly, in this instance we see that by jumping in and helping, they only prolonged a difficult situation and harmed more than helped.

> RECOGNIZE THAT JUMPING IN AND HELPING YOUR ADULT CHILD MAY ONLY PROLONG THE PROBLEM AND DO MORE HARM THAN GOOD.

Had Ralph and Margaret said no to Ted's requests for money and help earlier, much hardship could have been avoided, not only for their oldest son but also for other family members as well. Today, many years later, Ted has lost his license to practice and is still looking for handouts—free gifts of money, housing, and cars. His parents, long gone, contributed to this legacy of self-indulgence in their son.

Saying No Teaches Personal Responsibility

Raised in a loving home, Paul married a young woman his parents did not approve of. In spite of that, Phil and Eve, his parents, after recovering from the hurt and disappointment they felt, decided to back off and let him live his life.

A few months after the wedding, Paul's new wife, Renee, needed surgery. Paul called his father for help.

"Dad, I hate to ask, but could you float us a loan?"

Phil asked, "Are you all right? What's it for?"

"I'm okay. Things are just tight."

"Let me talk to your mother, and we'll get back to you."

When Phil and Eve discussed it, they disagreed but finally said they would lend the money this once.

Again, the following month, the second call came. "Mom, we're having a really rough time. Do you think you could lend us another 200?"

"Two hundred dollars, Paul? What's going on?"

"Please, Mom? I wouldn't ask if it weren't really important."

Again, Phil and Eve lent him the money.

"I'll pay it back as soon as I can," Paul promised.

The next call was more urgent. Paul's new wife was in the hospital for anxiety. They had no medical insurance. They needed more money.

"Another $200—for Renee's medications."

Paul's parents urged him to come for a visit, to talk. Paul promised he would as soon as he could.

The next call was even more desperate. "Mom, we got evicted. Renee wanted to move in with her father so we could get back on our feet, but when we got to San Francisco, he wouldn't let us in."

"Paul, didn't you talk with him before you drove all the way to San Francisco?"

"Renee did. She said he told her to come, but when we got here, he said we couldn't. We don't have any place to stay. Can we stay with you?"

Phil and Eve lived in San Jose, an hour south of San Francisco. "What about your job, Paul?"

"I had to quit it."

Phil and Eve realized they couldn't keep "fixing" their son's problems. He had made an independent adult choice, and he needed to find an adult solution. They had to ask themselves if they had taught their son how to handle the real world of suffering, conflict, and disappointment. Maybe they hadn't, but there was no time like the present to start.

"Paul, we love you very much, but we can't help you again." Those words were the hardest ones they ever spoke to their son. But they knew that it was time for some "tough" love. It was time their son found his own strength and resources for life's challenges.

They continued to let Paul know they loved him. They listened when he was upset, offered advice when asked, and gave him unconditional love. This was not an easy task, to take a step back and take their hands off. Paul's parents knew their son needed to rediscover God and His unfailing love. By stepping away and not "fixing" his problems, they gave God the opportunity to become more real in Paul's life.

> BY STEPPING AWAY AND NOT FIXING YOUR CHILD'S PROBLEMS, YOU GIVE GOD THE OPPORTUNITY TO BECOME MORE REAL TO YOUR CHILD.

In time, Paul stood on his own two feet and worked through his problems. He even thanked his parents for taking a "hard line" with him.

When a parent has to say no, it often involves financial issues. Lending money that's never paid back seems to be a universal complaint of parents. One way to avoid that is to present your adult child with a coupon book of payment stubs. Each month he or she mails the appropriate stub to you with the payment. If your child doesn't comply, "no" will be all he or she hears in the future.

Then there are the young adults who expect and ask for help all the time. Do we jump in and fix things because they ask? Do we write a check, bail them out, or lend them the car—again?

A Softer No

"Jason has the kind of personality where asking for money all the time is not a problem," Peggy explained. "We've had to learn to say no, and he's stopped asking so often. One thing my husband and I do, though, is that if we know he's doing his best to meet obligations, we'll do something for him and his family above and beyond the call of duty," she said, smiling. "We'll treat them to a movie or take the kids for ice cream. Then they know we love and support them, but we're not going to be their own personal ATM."

Every situation is different and requires fresh wisdom, ardent listening, and sensitive discernment.

The Power of Consequences

Leslie's son Mike lost his driver's license due to reckless driving. He was attending college and living at home and had just been hired to work at a restaurant. The first day he was scheduled to work, a mere 45 minutes before he was due to report, he asked Leslie if she could drive him to work.

Leslie thought about it and said, "Mike, I *could* drive you, but I don't think that would be helping you at all. You need to learn the consequences of your actions. You will have to either take a bus or ride your bike to work."

Her son opted to ride his bike. Leslie admitted to me that it was very hard to do this, since it was a long distance through heavy traffic. And to top it off, the worst happened —he was hit by a van, suffered severe knee injuries, and had three surgeries.

I asked Leslie if she felt guilty about it. She said, "No, I really don't. I believe the right and loving thing to do was teach him about personal responsibility. This whole incident did teach him that. He has gotten his act together since then in spite of the accident."

Afraid to Say No

Maybe you face requests from your adult children that are making you feel burdened or resentful. Your son asks you at the last minute to watch his children this weekend so he and his wife can have some rest and relaxation, when they went away less than a month ago. Or your daughter's family wants to borrow the RV again after returning it dirty the last time. Perhaps you're asked for business favors—to help your son's friend get a job with a client or to hire someone to work for you.

Whatever the requests, there comes a time when we know we need to say no. Maybe we're afraid of the response we'll receive from our grown children if we say no. Will they write us off? Stop calling? Be angry and withhold the grandchildren's visits? How *do* we say no?

Be honest. When your answer is no, it should come with good reasons to support it, and you should be open to rea-

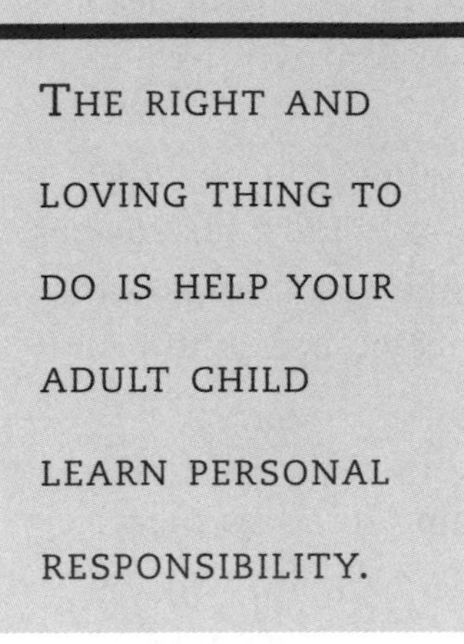

sonable questions. You can tell your son that you enjoy caring for the grandchildren but that you have a golf tournament to play in, dinner plans with friends, or the church social on Sunday. What's the best way to do that?

"A gentle answer turns away wrath, But a harsh word stirs up anger. The tongue of the wise makes knowledge acceptable, But the mouth of fools spouts folly" (Prov. 15:1-2, NASB). Gently suggest he give you more notice in the future, or tell him you'll be able to baby-sit only one weekend each month because you have other social commitments.

It's important to be clear—along with being reasonable and gentle—when denying your adult child's request to borrow your new motor home. If you've decided not to lend out your new vehicle anymore, you need to let him or her know that. But how, you say?

"Simply let your 'Yes' be 'Yes,' and your 'No,' 'No;' anything beyond this comes from the evil one" (Matt. 5:37). You might say something like "Dad and I bought the RV for our retirement, and we've decided to be careful about how much it's used. We figure we'll take it easy for the next few years so we won't be needing to buy another one for a long time."

Try to help find an alternative so their desired goal for a trip can be attained. Suggest solutions. Tell them about the RV dealer who rents used vehicles. Just because you say no doesn't mean the doors are closed. They simply must find another solution besides Mom and Dad.

Saying No Is Best for You

Pete and Jan finally launched their last child, a son, out into the business world. After the initial sadness of seeing the last of their children leave, they began to enjoy life as a twosome again. They rearranged the bedrooms to suit their new life and started taking trips, having date nights, and doing more entertaining in their home. Their daughter, Michelle, 27, after working as a waitress at various vacation resorts, earned her credential as a teacher and then found she really wasn't enjoying her job. She quit and went to school to become a masseuse. After a year, she didn't like that either. Finally she decided she knew what she wanted to do. She would go back to school, get a master's degree in psychology, and become a therapist. Only this time she asked Mom and Dad not only to foot the bill but also to provide her housing as well.

"I can do massages for extra cash," she offered, "but I won't be able to work full-time. The course work is really intense."

Pete and Jan, after praying about it, agreed that they had to tell Michelle no. They explained their position clearly, gently, reasonably—they were preparing for retirement; financial issues aside, they enjoyed their lifestyle of just the two of them. After their three children left, they had adapted their home to fit their needs. To have Michelle move home would mean dismantling their home office and filling their garage with the office furniture and all of Michelle's things.

They felt that if Michelle wanted to make another career

change badly enough, she would find a way to make it work. They also felt saying no would help their daughter understand and respect them better.

> THERE MAY COME A TIME WHEN YOU KNOW YOU NEED TO SAY NO.

The good news is that Michelle did make it work. Over the next year she found extra jobs and saved for her education. She found a roommate and started graduate school the next fall.

Because Pete and Jan explained their position in a kind, compassionate way that firmly expressed that their lifestyle is important and to be respected, their goal for a healthy relationship was maintained. Their saying no was reasonable.

It's important to remember that the opportunity of saying no is just that—an opportunity. Because being asked for something is one way our words can influence our children's lives.

Saying No Is an Opportunity to Influence

Steve's son asked, "Dad, can you and Mom watch the kids on Sundays? Sherrie and I have a chance to work together at a real estate office and make some extra cash on weekends."

Steve was surprised his son would ask this, because in their family they had taught their kids to honor the Lord's Day by not working unnecessarily.

Steve said, "No, son, because at the end of your life how much extra money you made when you were 30 won't matter at all. How much time you spent with your family and how much time you spent with the Lord will."

Saying no was a good way for Steve to remind his son about what's most important.

Sometimes saying no is just what our children need to hear to toughen them up. Conversely, we see what happens when a permissive "yes" wins out over a difficult but more loving "no."

A Biblical Example: The Apostle Paul

In 2 Cor. 12:7-10, we read the story of Paul, who had experienced great visions and revelations of God. "To keep me from becoming conceited because of these surpassingly great revelations, there was given me a thorn in my flesh. . . . Three times I pleaded with the Lord to take it away from me" (vv. 7-8).

God's response to Paul was no. The thorn in his flesh was for his own good, to keep him from pride and arrogance, to remind him of his place in the kingdom. God the Father knew that no was the best for Paul.

Parenting Pointers

In saying no, giving less, you can take the following steps:

1. Remember the consequences of *not* saying no.
   - Listen, assess, pray, discern.
2. Saying no teaches personal responsibility.
   - Offer help in other ways.
   - Demonstrate love when saying no.
   - Explain why you're saying no.
   - Remember that God says no too.
   - Be clear.

- Be gentle and kind.
- Be honest.
- Suggest possible alternatives.
- Saying no is an opportunity to influence.

3. Your adult children need to understand and respect your needs.

- Offer to baby-sit or help when convenient.
- When saying no, explain what your needs are.
- Your situation—retirement, financial, and health concerns—should be voiced and respected.

5

Establishing New Boundaries

Love your neighbor as yourself (Lev. 19:18).

JOHN and Merilee didn't know until the Christmas holidays that their son's college studies were "going poorly." Bryan had always been a responsible child, and they were more than a little surprised to learn the news, but they sent him back to school with admonitions to try harder to pull up those grades. He assured them he would. Believers in extending grace and second chances, they trusted Bryan.

But a few weeks later when grades came out, they realized the extent of their son's "doing poorly"—he was on academic probation!

How could this be? Bryan was a good student. They had worked hard to help him get into this prestigious, sought-after college of his choice, and now he was flunking out? They were bewildered and confused.

When Merilee spoke to him over the phone, she asked about the "Incomplete" in his music class. "Why don't you do make-up work?" she asked.

"I can't," Bryan answered glibly. "I was supposed to attend a concert and write a paper, but I didn't make it to the concert."

It was at precisely that moment Merilee realized that she and her husband had to change their parenting practices. They had extended enough grace. It might have worked in high school when he lived at home, but that was no longer the case. No more second chances, no more gentle reminders to do better. Bryan needed to suffer the consequences of his actions.

They knew that love and limits go together, so after that moment of enlightenment, they set new, distinct boundaries. They told him that if he failed any classes, he would have to finance the rest of his college education on his own.

Fortunately, the story has a happy ending. Bryan brought his grades up. He knew his parents meant business because they had established boundaries with him earlier in his life.

Codependent and Needing Boundaries

Kent often hangs out at his parents' house, vacations with them, drops off his laundry, and eats many meals there. He's their closest confidant, sharing everything with them. At 31, he hasn't found his career niche and has no savings, no retirement plan, and no health insurance.

Kent's other adult relationships are dysfunctional. He chooses "black sheep" friends. He seems unable to commit to a member of the opposite sex or to a career.

Often his finances are a problem. He has large and multiple credit card balances and usually is behind on his taxes. Although he's earning his own way, he never thinks of the future.

This scenario occurs in friendly, loving families, where things are so nice it's hard to leave. *It doesn't look like a problem because everyone gets along so well*. All the family members are happy with one another. On the surface, these do not appear to be serious problems. But adult children like Kent who have not separated from their parents are still under parental protection, and it's his parents' job to think about the future. By allowing this behavior to continue, Mark and Suzanne are symbolically keeping Kent from emotionally leaving home.

In this example, we see a classic lack of boundaries. What are boundaries? Boundaries are a personal property line that delineates the things for which we're responsible. Boundaries define who we are and who we are not. They're for self-protection and for taking personal responsibility for our own needs.

From Indulgent to Accountable

Ric Edelman, a radio broadcaster, relates this story:

A listener, Bob, once called my radio show. "Ric, what should I do with my money? I have $24,000 and no debt." I was impressed.

Most of the 20-somethings I know are broke and have lots of credit cards. Bob said the bulk of his money was an inheritance and it was just sitting in his bank account.

I asked him about his monthly expenses. To my surprise, he said, "Oh, I spend about two hundred dollars a month." Bob, 23 and a college graduate, lives at home.

Upon graduation, he became an official member of "The Boomerang Generation."

When Bob graduated, he moved back home. His total monthly spending of $200 goes to whatever he wants—

> YOU MAY REACH A MOMENT WHEN YOU REALIZE IT'S TIME TO CHANGE YOUR PARENTING PRACTICES.

parties, going to the movies, eating out with the guys, and other activities of the financially secure. Bob is able to participate in these avocations because "someone else" does his laundry, cooks his meals, and pays the bills.

Why should Bob move out when he can live in a 3,000-square-foot home in the suburbs? Let's face it: Bob's got a great thing going here and the operative initials are M-O-M and D-A-D.

Parents must recognize that at 23, these "kids" are adults who need to act like adults. Parents are not doing their adult children any favors by coddling and protecting them against the cold, cruel realities of life.[1]

Ric's advice to these parents is to set boundaries by charging Bob rent, as would any other landlord. They should collect an amount equal to (a) what Bob would pay elsewhere or (b) what Mom and Dad would charge if Bob were a stranger.

If they were to charge $1,000 a month, two things would happen: Bob would get a job to pay for it, and he would move out. Both are exactly what he needs to do if he's to develop and thrive in our society.

Setting limits has to do with telling the truth. By establishing new boundaries and obligations, parents help their adult children take responsibility for their own lives, and in the process, they'll learn to respect their parents' needs as well.

Boundaries Enable Choices

Susie respected her parents' wishes over her own. She would return from a visit to her parents' home only to suffer deep depression. When asked to describe her most recent trip home, Susie told of social gatherings with old friends and family around the dinner table. "It was fun," she said, "especially when it was only family."

When asked what she meant by *only* family, she explained how her parents would invite some of her friends over, and in front of her friends they would make subtle remarks about how wonderful it must be to have a "hands-on" role in raising grandchildren; then they would exclaim about all the community activities her friends were engaged in, how wonderful Susie would be at those activities if only she lived there.

Susie soon discovered that when she returned home, she felt as if she were bad for living where she did. She had a nagging sense that she really should do what her parents wanted her to do.

Susie had a common problem. She had made choices *on the outside*. She had moved away from family to pursue a career. She paid her owns bills, married, and had a child. But on the *inside* things were different. She did not have emotional permission to be a separate person, make free choices about her life, and be free of guilt when she did not do what her parents wanted.

In the book *Boundaries*, by Henry Cloud and John Townsend, the authors point out that a problem like Susie's is that she does not really "own" herself.[2]

People who own their lives don't feel guilty when they make choices about where they're going. They take other people into consideration, but when they make choices based on the wishes of others, they're choosing out of love, not guilt.

As parents, how can we help our adult children "own" themselves? First, we can understand the importance of setting boundaries, then enforcing them.

But what about our fears of an unhappy ending? Is it possible our child will become angry at our boundaries and attack or withdraw from us? The hard reality is that we have no control over the response of others, especially our adult children. Some will welcome our boundaries; others will hate them.

Sticking to the Boundaries—the Only Way

Peggy tells her story of setting boundaries and sticking to them:

> I reached across my pillow and groped in the dark for the ringing telephone. "Hello," I mumbled, trying to have coherent thought.
>
> "Mom?"
>
> Middle-of-the-night phone calls always bring a sense of dread. This time there was an urgent note in my 24-year-old son's voice that caused my blood to run cold.
>
> "Christian?" Wide-awake now, I bolted upright. "What's wrong? What time is it?"
>
> "It's about two o'clock, and I'm in jail."
>
> My heart did a flip-flop; I could hardly breathe as a horri-

BOUNDARIES DEFINE WHO YOU ARE AND WHO YOU ARE NOT.

fying vision of why he might be there flashed through my mind.

"I need you to come and get me out, Mom."

"What happened?"

"I missed a court date for a speeding ticket. I was picked up on a bench warrant."

The light on the other side of the bed clicked on, and my husband, Albert, turned toward me. "What's going on?"

I explained in a rush and ended with "We have to go get him."

Albert put his hand on my arm and captured my panicked eyes. "We can't do that. We agreed."

Yes, we had agreed. All three of our children knew they would be expected to pay the consequences for irresponsible behavior. When they were young, holding them accountable was a lot easier, because we pretty-much controlled their activities. With adult children who make their own decisions, the consequences of their behavior can often be more severe—for the parent as well as the child.

"But this is different," I said. "Jail is not a safe place."

"And he's an adult. What would we be teaching him if we bail him out now? We've told him consistently that he needs to take care of previous speeding tickets and drive more responsibly."

Ah, the voice of reason. "You're right," I said, wondering how I could leave my son in a cell with drug dealers, rapists, and murderers. He wasn't a criminal, for heaven's sake. I swallowed past the lump in my throat and tried to get my fear under control. Then I put the phone back to my ear and explained to Christian why we couldn't help him.

"Mom, please!"

The desperation in his voice brought tears to my eyes that overflowed down my cheeks. I looked at Albert, wanting to change my mind. "I—"

"I'll take it from here." Gently, he pried the phone from my grasp.

Please take care of Christian, Lord. I knew in my heart it was the right decision, but I felt sick to my stomach. It was the hardest "no" I ever said.

I can't say that Christian is truly grateful for his nine days in jail, even today, but at least he can now see the value in the pain. He was "scared straight" out of procrastination that could land him in trouble. No way does he want to go through that experience again.

In this instance, boundaries and consequences served to teach personal responsibility. By forcing their child to take ownership for his actions, Albert and Peggy initiated his responsibility for taking care of himself rather than placing the burden on someone else.

Cloud and Townsend state that our adult children should hold these convictions:

- My success or failure in life largely depends on me.
- Though I'm to look to God and others for comfort and instruction, I alone am responsible for my choices.
- Though I'm deeply affected by my significant relationships throughout my life, I can't blame my problems on anyone but myself.
- Though I'll sometimes fail and need support, I can't depend on some other responsible individual to constantly bail me out of spiritual, emotional, financial, or relational crises.[3]

The sense of "my life is up to me" is grounded in God's

desire that we take responsibility for our lives, as taught in Matt. 25:14-30.

Boundaries for Mutual Respect

There also comes the time when we parents need to accept and honor the boundaries of our adult children. Family psychologist John Rosemond writes a column for the Knight Ridder News Service:

> *Question*: We have a 20-year-old daughter who feels we have no right to restrict her behavior. She refuses to go to church with us and often stays out past curfew. I think we should start enforcing the rules or tell her to leave. My daughter is very responsible, and communication between us is usually good. She contends that when she turned 19 she "graduated" from having to follow our rules. Am I being unreasonable?
>
> *Answer*: I take no pleasure in informing people of such things, but you are your own worst enemy.
>
> There is a difference between not liking decisions an adult child is making and trying to control them. If the issue is simply a matter of who's right, you are. Being right does not justify your hyper vigilant attempts to micromanage your daughter. All you've managed to do is create a power struggle that—now listen up!—you cannot possibly win.

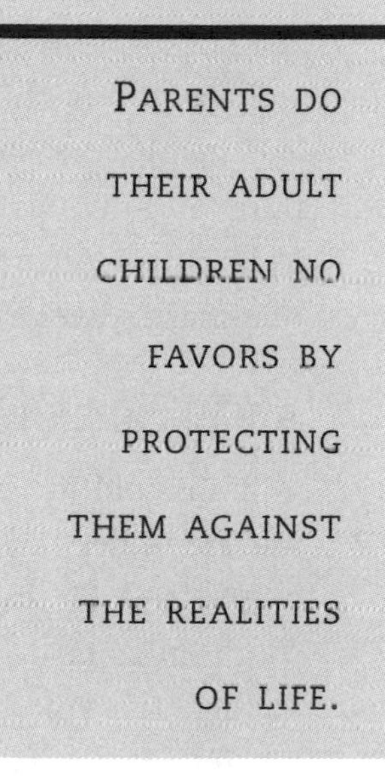

> Your daughter definitely does not need to be living at home any longer. She is responsible enough to support herself and obviously does not want to abide by anyone else's rules. Therefore, she needs to be emancipated. Not ejected, mind you, but emancipated, joyously.[4]

While I don't completely agree with Mr. Rosemond's advice, this situation is a good example of establishing boundaries for *mutual* respect. The parents need to set boundaries to retain the atmosphere they want in their home, and their daughter, an adult, needs to be able to live her own life, make her own rules, but in her own residence.

Setting boundaries with adult children can be a fearsome task, but a necessary one, both for us as parents and for the welfare of our children. Establishing limits, telling the truth, and being consistent will, over time, produce the responsibility and ownership we want our children to have in order to face their future. By making the difficult choices in setting boundaries, we're demonstrating selfless, godly love.

A Biblical Example: the Rich Young Man

Jesus told the rich young man a hard truth about eternal life. He understood that the man worshiped money. So he set boundaries. He told the young man to give it away, to make room in his heart for God. The results were not encouraging: "When the young man heard this, he went away sad, because he had great wealth" (Matt. 19:22).

Jesus didn't manipulate the situation. He knew the young man had to know whom to worship, so He let him walk away. We as parents can do no less. We can't manipulate our children into swallowing our boundaries by sugarcoating them. Boundaries are a litmus test for the quality of our relationship with our children.

Parenting Pointers

In establishing boundaries, you can take the following steps:

1. Understand that boundaries are for self-protection, assuming personal responsibility, and for self-definition.

2. Adjust boundaries with adult children:
    - Financial
    - Relational
    - Societal
    - Professional

3. Acknowledge that their lives are their responsibility, not yours.

4. Realize that boundaries help adult children respect their parents as separate, autonomous adults.

5. Accept that you have no control over your adult children's responses to your boundary-setting.
    - Be willing to accept the outcome of healthy boundary-setting.
    - Respect yourself by sticking to your boundaries (as Jesus did).
    - Trust God in the process.

6. Remember the goal. Setting boundaries will help build stronger, healthier relationships with your adult children.

6

Fine-Tuning Communication

Reckless words pierce like a sword, but the tongue of the wise brings healing (Prov. 12:18).

IN the first chapter we talked about living beyond giving advice. At the heart of our wanting to continue guiding and instructing our children is the issue of control. If we're going to succeed in our goal of promoting a healthy adult relationship with them, then we need to consider a shift in the way we communicate.

Respecting Our Adult Children

For my friend Sue, clues that she needed to change were right in her face.

A few months after her son got married, he and his bride invited her over for dinner for the first time. As they chatted around the table, her son leaned back in his chair so that the front two legs came off the floor.

"Stop leaning back like that," Sue scolded.

"I don't have to—this isn't your house," he quipped. With a chuckle he added, "You don't know how long I've wanted to be able to say that to you!"

That served as a gentle but clear reminder to Sue that her son now had his own household and could make his own rules. She says, "It was time to begin treating him as my adult peer instead of as my youngest child."

When our children were young, we were constantly correcting and guiding their behavior, and our methods became ingrained within us. Fortunately, our children often let us know—sometimes subtly, sometimes not so subtly—when it is time for us to refine our methods.

Small things—a joking phrase, a gentle word, or even a pointed barb—can make us suddenly aware of the need to modify our behavior toward our now-adult children.

- Are we badgering them during each phone call?
- Do we still give endless advice?
- Do we grill them with questions when they come to visit?
- Do we put them on guilt trips about not calling or coming home more often?
- Are we lecturing, judging, expecting, interrupting, rolling our eyes, displaying a tone of voice, and crossing our arms, leaving the room in frustration and dismissal?

Rather: ask, listen actively, show respect, use "I" messages, repeat back, seek to understand, be empathic.

Communication Advice from Joyce Brothers

When our adult kids finally do ask for our wisdom, we should be ready. There's an art to it.

> THE GREATER BURDEN IS ON THE PARENT TO BRING ABOUT HEALING AND CHANGE IN A TROUBLED RELATIONSHIP WITH AN ADULT CHILD.

Listen with your mind and your body. Make eye contact and use body language that indicates you are engaged in what they are saying. Nod and comment. Only ask questions that expand on the problem. For example: "What's going on with your boss?"

Hear the person out before jumping in with a solution. Find out what's wanted. After hearing the whole story, ask, "What do you think you should do?" This allows you to gauge the intention in asking for advice. If your child keeps venting, he or she wants support, not advice.

Don't be discouraged if listening is the most you can do. Clarify what needs fixing. Zero in on the specific problem. Ask, "What would you like to change?" or "What would you like to accomplish?" Guide your child to clearly define the problem. Don't label it yourself. Reframing statements can help to clarify matters. "Did I hear you say . . .?"

Then, you can safely say, "Do you have any ideas in mind?" or "What do you think might work?"

When asked pointedly, "What would you do?" make sure you don't suggest changing what can't be changed. Finally, accept your own limits. Serious problems like depression, drug addiction, domestic abuse, or suicide threats all require professional help. Even when the problems aren't that serious and we give our advice and suggestions, doesn't mean it will be acted upon.[1]

As parents, of course, we know that one of the main things we want to do is "fix it." We want to make everything better, to ease the pain, to make life flow more smoothly. But there comes a time with young adults when fixing things or taking matters into our own hands just isn't the best tack to take.

Listen with Respect

"I give up. He simply won't listen!" said Gloria, 24, about her dad. It was a common complaint. The situation finally came to a head one weekend after her dad helped her move her things out of her apartment into a storage unit. She had specifically asked him to stack the boxes a particular way so she could get into those boxes at a later time.

He simply stacked the boxes the way *he* wanted without considering her request. She claims he didn't listen.

He said he had no choice because there wasn't room to do it her way.

Meanwhile, Mom wanted to shake both of them. She knew that even though her daughter was annoyed at where Dad put the boxes, the real problem was that Gloria feels discounted and ignored when Dad doesn't listen to her wishes.

A better solution would have been for Dad to discuss the space problem with his daughter and let her make the decision about where to place things. Yes, it may have taken longer, but it would have done wonders for their relationship.

While Mom can see the problem clearly and they can't, she continues to pray, asking the Holy Spirit to speak to both of them, to break down their stubbornness so they can come together in forgiveness and understanding.

As mature adults, the greater burden is on parents to bring about healing and change.

Adjusting the Lenses

For Jill, the signs that her communication technique with her sons needed changing finally became clear only after a long, harried summer.

"I was blessed with identical twin sons. My boys were busy, entertaining, and wonderfully wild. I knew from the beginning that my sons did not 'belong' to me. I knew my job was to raise them to leave home with humble confidence to make a difference in their world."

As the boys were beginning sixth grade, Jill's husband deserted the family, leaving behind their sons and putting their futures in her hands. As the years passed, the boys and their mom grew very close. Their house was the place to find a cold Coke, brownies, and a parent ready to listen, no matter the hour. During the high school years, they seldom had disagreements, but when they did, they were settled quickly and without grudges.

After their freshman year in college, the twins returned home for the summer. Remember that they rarely argued in high school? In two and a half short months, they more than made up for it.

Jill says, "I had rules—they didn't. I work out of my home and needed to maintain normal hours—they didn't. I kept the air conditioning at 78; they turned it down to 68, but I was paying the electric bill—they weren't. After the first two weeks I was ready to resign as their mother!

"Then, at 3 A.M. one morning, I was lying awake wondering if and when they were coming home when I realized my urges to resign from motherhood weren't off the mark but right on target. If I was going to be a successful mother at this stage in their lives, it was time to step aside from mothering—or 'smothering,' as the boys called it.

"The next morning, I made a promise to begin looking at the boys as men, not little boys."

That summer full of experiences opened Jill's eyes to the fact that she had to change her parenting techniques and communication style.

To Speak or Not to Speak

"I've 'graduated' three adult children and I've learned plenty along the way," Marlene says. "I remember a time when I was troubled by a particular situation. I prayed about it and mentally wrestled with what I should do. Should I say something? Should I say nothing? I finally talked to a friend about my concern.

"She said, 'Marlene, if we say nothing, our children interpret our silence as either approval or a sign that we don't care.' Then she encouraged me not to overreact with the 'jump-down-your-throat' approach, which can lead to anger and rebellion.

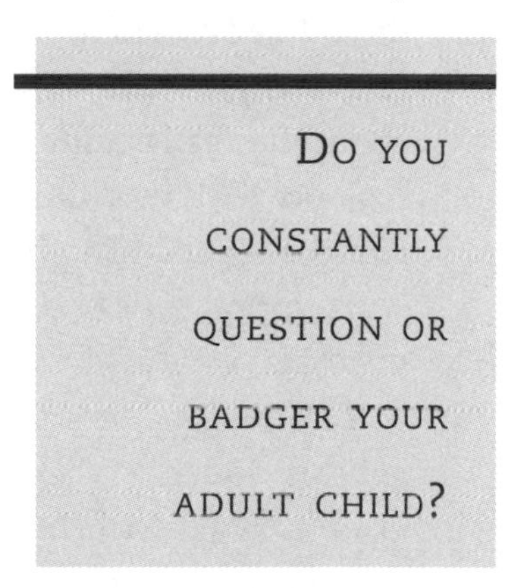

"I thought long and hard about what she had said. Then I prayed for the right opportunity to have a conversation with my daughter.

"It wasn't long before she invited me to go for a walk. I knew this was my opportunity. Although I can't recall the exact conversation, it went something like this: 'I understand that at your age, it's not my job to control you. I want to assure you that this isn't my intention. As your mom, I care deeply and want nothing but the best for you. I want to share some of my concerns about . . . Have you considered . . .? What about . . .?' The questions continued, interspersed with her responses. I finished by reminding her that I would always love her regardless of the outcome on this subject, and I gave her a warm hug.

"It was a hard conversation. I had knots in my stomach, and I had no guarantees of the outcome, so I prayed and waited. I knew I had done the right thing."

Too Many Questions?

Consider all the "helpful" questions we ask our adult children. I know when our daughters moved to Hawaii last fall, I found myself unconsciously giving them the third degree about the many things that needed to be done. Only it wasn't my move. It was theirs. They had the situation well under control, even though this was a complicated undertaking with shipping a car, dealing with freight charges, getting estimates, and so on.

I know my questions, ticking off my checklist—"Did you get this done?" or "Did you remember to call so and so?" or "Don't forget to bring that paper"—for the most part were appreciated. But there were moments when I heard an exasperated sigh or tone of voice that tipped me off that I was being overbearing. Fortunately for me, I picked up on the hints and backed off with my questions. If they forgot something or didn't fill out a form correctly, then they would deal with it. Another way would have been to simply ask *one* question: "Did you get all of the boxes shipped?" or "Is there anything I can do to help?"

While acknowledging the need to back off with our freely-given wisdom, what about those times when the stakes are particularly high and involve their physical, emotional, or financial security? It might be almost impossible for a responsible parent to sit back and remain silent. What do we do? Depending on your relationship with your child, one way might be to ask permission to offer suggestions. If the response is "I don't need your help," then we must respect that and not interfere.

Another mom adds to that: "Before I say something to or do something for one of my sons or his wife, I ask myself this question: 'Is what I am about to say or do something I would say to or do for a friend?'

"Using that question as a guideline has helped me bite my tongue at times and has ultimately given me the joy of a great relationship with both of my married sons and their families."

Allowing for Differences

My friend Bonnie admitted one of her barriers to mutual understanding: "The biggest realization I've had is that when I struggle with decisions my children make, it's so much about me wanting them to be happy in the way I perceive happiness—from my experience, my viewpoint, my own struggles. What I've had to learn is that they're seeing things from *their* experiences, *their* viewpoints, *their* struggles. Happiness to them is not necessarily the same as it is to me."

A frequent topic of conversation with her daughter Margaret, aged 28, is marriage versus long-term relationships. Margaret is quite happy to settle for a relationship with no strings attached. Bonnie, on the other hand, used to remind her that marriage is intended for a happy union.

After Bonnie realized that this was how *she* perceived happiness and not necessarily the way Margaret sees the issue, she had to back off when her daughter would become quiet or upset. She now will preface comments with words like "I say this because I want you to be happy the way I perceive it." She says that when she does that, Margaret seems to understand that her mother is not trying to live her life for her.

Extending Grace While Disapproving

Hank and Darcy's daughter Missy had been a perfect child growing up. She was an excellent student and athlete, was attractive, had many friends, and was a joy to all who knew her. She graduated from college with honors and moved to a nearby town for a job in her chosen field.

After she settled in, she invited her parents to come for a visit. When Hank and Darcy arrived, they were shocked to see Missy living with Chuck, a young man they had met during her college years. The two young people had talked about the possibility of marriage, but they had agreed that they weren't ready for the commitment. Instead, they decided to try living together.

Fortunately, Hank and Darcy were able to handle themselves maturely. They listened to the young couple in stark bewilderment and realized that Missy and Chuck knew all too well what their feelings were. They could even see that the young couple had carefully planned their presentation and were ready for the parents' reactions.

Hank and Darcy gently asked the appropriate questions and made known their concerns and wishes, lovingly but without being judgmental or unpleasant, even though their hearts were breaking. They experienced how difficult it was to be civil to their child's partner even though they knew to be unpleasant would be a serious mistake that could drive Missy away. Also, if she married Chuck, their future relationship with the young couple would be damaged.

When they left for home after dinner that night, Hank and Darcy cried together but decided that maintaining their goal of a relationship with Missy and Chuck was the most critical factor.

In the following months, they spent a lot of time with Missy and Chuck. Hank and Darcy prayed fervently about the situation and asked friends to pray with them.

One day Missy and Chuck invited her parents to come for dinner. Over dessert the young couple asked their advice about plans for marriage. They revealed that the parents' kindness and love to them had much to do with the decision to follow their wishes and example.

Hank and Darcy returned home thanking God for answering their prayers while being grateful that as parents they hadn't said or done anything to alienate their daughter.

They shared with friends that it's far better to treat your child's significant other as a likable person and show common courtesies to him or her. In spite of how difficult this is, with God's grace we can behave with love and kindness even though we don't approve of their behavior. You can still appreciate the person while not approving the behavior. The tone of voice, a handshake greeting, and occasional hugs all can build up the person.

Tools for Fine-Tuning

In refining our methods of communication, there are many other tools and skills we can develop. Affirming even the briefest moment our adult child displays Christlike character encourages him or her more than we realize. A parent's spoken blessing is tremendously powerful and can build strength that lasts a lifetime and even offer direction.

In *The Gift of the Blessing*, authors Gary Smalley and John Trent write,

> Written words become a lifelong legacy for a child to keep. In a letter you can express your pride in them, or share what you're learning from the Scriptures, or what you're doing that fills them in on your life. Whether they're waiting in the mail line in the military, reaching into their mailbox at school, or thumbing through their letters in their own home or apartment, written words of blessing from a parent are incredibly powerful.[2]

IT'S BETTER TO SHOW COMMON COURTESY TO YOUR CHILD'S SIGNIFICANT OTHER EVEN IF YOU DON'T REALLY APPROVE OF THE RELATIONSHIP.

In an earlier chapter we discussed the importance of understanding personality differences. Here we need to look at male and female differences. Men speak what Gary Smalley and John Trent call the "language of the head."[3] Call it "fact talk"—it means men often enjoy dealing with the hard, cold facts—clinical black-and-white thinking. Women, on the other hand, generally speak a "language of the heart" and are comfortable with both facts and feelings. Women are more interested in details, in relationships, and in expressing the love they feel.[4]

One communication skill that is particularly effective in bridging both gender and age barriers is the use of emotional word pictures. Stories or objects are used to simultaneously activate the emotions and intellect of a person. In so doing, they cause the person to *experience* our words, not just to hear them. Jesus was a master of this technique—in fact, it was His primary method of communication. An emotional word picture can sharpen and extend your parenting skills by maximizing your words. It also helps you whittle many problems down to size.

In the following example of an emotional word picture, it's the daughter (Leslie) who's reaching out, trying to bridge the communication gap with her father through a personal letter. The father, Steve, has filed for divorce, is seeing another woman, and lives across town. After a long, hectic day at work, Steve glanced at the pile of mail before him. His eyes caught sight of a personal letter. Looking closer, he recognized Leslie's handwriting. Instead of finding a card or note, Steve found an emotional word picture of how his leaving had devastated her and the family.

Dear Dad,

> I feel like our family has been riding in a nice car for a long time. It's the kind that has every option inside and not a scratch on the outside.
>
> But over the years the car has developed some problems. It's smoking a lot, the wheels wobble, and the seat covers are ripped. But it's still a great car—or at least it could be. With a little work, I know it could run for years.
>
> It was nighttime and we had just turned the corner near our house. Suddenly, we all looked up and saw another car, out of control, heading straight for us. Mom

tried to swerve out of the way, but the other car still smashed into us.

The thing is, Dad, just before being hit, we could see that you were driving the other car. And we saw something else: sitting next to you was another woman.

We were rushed to the emergency ward.

She goes on to describe their injuries, the pain and agony, and how bad it was. She closes by saying, "At night when the hospital is really quiet, they push Brian and me into Mom's room, and we all talk about you. We talk about how much we loved driving with you and how we wish you were here with us now."

This emotional word picture of how his leaving affected the family touched Steve deeply. When all the cajoling, pleading, and begging for him to return home didn't work, this image broke through to his heart. We parents can use a tool like this to reach intimacy and communication with our adult children.

Even though we often feel that we're walking a tightrope in dealing with adult children, I'm confident we can be successful in fine-tuning our communication patterns. It takes persistence and determination to implement new techniques as well as temper old patterns. Treating our children as friends, offering them the respect we would a friend, honoring their individuality and uniqueness, and finding new ways to bridge gaps in communication will help build better bridges to understanding.

A Biblical Example: God's Communication Style

I'm struck by the various methods God uses throughout the Bible to communicate with us, His children. In the Old

Testament we see the burning bush, The Ark of the Covenant, the Cloud of His Presence, to name a few. He uses dreams, visions, voices, angels, even a donkey to get through to us. In the New Testament are signs, wonders, miracles, healings, divine revelations, and sometimes silence.

Parenting Pointers

In fine-tuning your relationship with your adult children, you can take the following steps:

1. Observe the clues:
   - A joking phrase
   - A gentle word
   - A pointed barb
   - An open, frank request
2. Ask yourself:
   - Do I still give unwanted advice, grill them, or interrupt?
   - Do I put them on guilt trips about their lack of calls or visits?
   - Am I critical? Or do I love them unconditionally?
   - Does my body language and tone of voice indicate that I'm listening?
   - Do I use "I" messages instead of "you" messages?
   - Do I find out what specifically they want and need from me?
   - Do I treat them as adults, as friends?
   - Do I pray about when to speak and when not to?
   - Do I ask permission to offer suggestions?
   - Am I allowing my adult children to live out their perceptions of happiness, not mine?

- Will my method of communication reach my goal of promoting a healthier, stronger relationship with my children?

7

Pointing Them to God

The righteous man leads a blameless life; blessed are his children after him (Prov. 20:7).

I was sound asleep when the phone rang. It was 4:17 A.M. on the digital clock.

"Hello?"

The line crackled in the distance. "Will you accept a collect call from . . . Megan?"

I sat bolt upright. "Yes, yes," I said quickly.

"Mom?" came the plaintive voice of our 22-year-old daughter. Before I could answer, deep, heaving sobs filled the phone lines for thousands of miles. It was only day number two of the long-awaited trip to Europe for Megan and our older daughter, Kim.

"Meg . . ." I tried to keep calm, even though my heart was now racing wildly and my palms were sweaty as I gripped the phone. Meanwhile, my husband flew out of bed to get to the extension in the next room.

"Meg." I repeated calmly. "Tell me what's wrong."

"We, we're stranded." More sobs.

"How?" my husband asked.

My mind raced—they had a rental car, plenty of traveler's checks, and credit cards. So how could they be stranded? A flash of anger mixed with fear for them. Had I not prayed for weeks before their trip, because I had been so nervous about this very thing happening? Matt. 21:22 played through my mind: "If you believe, you will receive whatever you ask for in prayer." *But I do believe, God! You know how hard I worked to give all my fears to you, Lord.* My grip on the phone tightened, waiting the forever seconds until she could compose herself to speak again.

HOW DO THINGS GO WRONG EVEN WHEN WE'VE PRAYED FOR EVERY ASPECT OF OUR CHILDREN'S LIVES?

"It's the car. It keeps stalling. We had to pull off the Autobahn. We're in a little German town. And Kim is sick. She's throwing up because she's so stressed about the car. No one will take credit cards or dollars, and we're hungry. We used up our phone card trying to call the rental car people back in Munich. We have to get to our next hostel or we'll lose our reservation. I'm sorry this is collect. I didn't know what else to do."

My husband and I both started talking at once. He let me go first. "Megan. First, take a deep breath. It's going to be okay. Forget about the reservations. You need to get the car situation solved first." I took a breath.

"But before you do anything, Meg, I want you to pray. Go back to the car to be with Kim and just sit there and pray. God has the solution for you."

We talked for a few more minutes, my husband encouraging and reassuring her that it would be all right and reminding them to call us back when they had a plan.

Hanging up and letting go of that fragile connection was so hard to do! I felt as if I was casting them adrift somehow. But there was nothing I could do from where I was except pray for their safety and well-being.

For weeks I had wrestled with letting them go to Europe together (not that I had any real say in the matter). I thought of how the president and vice president travel on separate planes—I always thought that was a superb idea. I finally relinquished my fears, releasing both daughters into God's hands, into His care and protection—at least until this fiasco.

How could this happen when we had prayed about every aspect of their travel? Not just "cover-it-all" prayers about health, safety, and so on, but I had also prayed about details, about the car they got, the roads they drove on, and for the people they met. You name it—I prayed about it.

Lord, I said now, *I know you have a plan here. Please help them to see it.*

My husband and I prayed again and then went online to try and get a better sense of where they were. Maybe we could call the rental car people. We brainstormed, trying to think of how we could help, if we could help. But in the end, there was little we could do but wait.

Five torturous hours passed. I had a temper tantrum with God. I cried, I railed. And finally, at 9:20 A.M. the phone rang again. In an instant, we were both on the phone.

This time Megan was chipper, almost jubilant. "You won't believe it! The baker we tried to buy bread from saw us sitting in the car and came out with his family to see if we needed help. The daughter spoke a little English, but mainly we used a lot of hand signals. They figured out that the car was the problem. So you know what they did? They took us to a nearby field and showed us how to drive the car! It turns out that European transmissions are different from the American or Japanese kinds we have in the states. Kim and I both learned and feel comfortable with the car now."

She continued on, excitedly. "Then they took us to a bank and translated for us so we could exchange money. And after that, they took us to a market so we could buy some groceries for our road trip. So now we're on our way to Salzburg."

Tears of relief and gratitude streamed down my face for that fine German family who rescued our daughters, and of course, to God, who prompted them to help. Joy, relief, and fatigue all at once overcame me. We hung up after asking them to call us later in the day to let us know they were still okay.

What a lesson this experience was for all of us! For me, trying to be Mommy to young adult daughters from halfway across the globe was a wake-up call that the role I had enjoyed for years was changing before my very eyes. God wants to become "Father" in every sense of the word to my now-grown children. He desires to be their perfect heavenly parent, to satisfy their needs—needs that my husband and I can never meet. It's time to relinquish, to surrender our desires and guidance to God.

Our daughters did call later, and the car was fine after they mastered the art of shifting a European transmission. God graciously showed me that He's more than capable of watching out for them.

We thought their adventures in Europe were under control, that the big lesson we needed to learn was behind us—but we were wrong.

A few days later, my husband received a call at work from our older daughter, Kim, this time from Rome. The previous night they had been lost for six hours trying to find their little hotel. The street wasn't listed on the map, if you can believe that. At 2 A.M. they finally checked in. After encountering a very rude clerk who disliked Americans, they went to their "room," which had holes in the floor covered by loose patches of linoleum, a nonfunctioning, filthy toilet, no shower, two beds that were unmade and soiled. Not only that, but also the room had a mysterious odd door leading to who-knows-where. Yet in spite of all that, in their exhaustion the girls decided they had no choice but to stay until morning. They barricaded the unknown door with furniture and slept on top of the sheets. In the morning, they had tiny bug bites all over them.

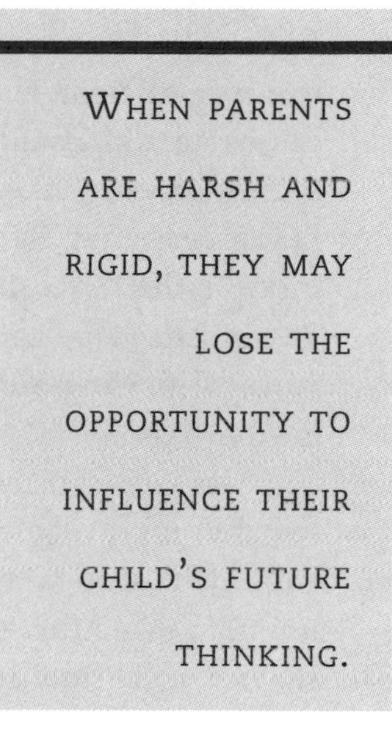

My husband prayed with Kim, encouraged her, and assured her that upon her return he would help her deal with the travel agent who booked that hotel.

For me, the big lesson of learning I had to let go and let God become their Source was only part of it. Months after the girls returned from their adventure in Europe, they each shared on separate occasions that their relationship with God had grown by leaps and bounds on that trip. "Mom, I *saw* God answering our prayers." "I never knew just how much God cared for *me* until that experience in Germany."

I asked God for forgiveness for being upset with Him for allowing this crisis. But more important, I realized we did do some things right. When faced with the crisis, our instinctive gut reaction was to pray. Our daughters saw this. Sure, as a family, they had seen us pray numerous times before. But this was different. They were on the other side of the planet, desperate and afraid. They saw that our response was the same—pray! And then they witnessed firsthand those prayers being answered. The lesson took on undisputable significance in their lives. I know that in the days ahead, when crisis strikes again—and it will—they'll remember the importance of praying and seeking God's wisdom before doing anything else.

I was vulnerable with my daughters when they returned. I shared my struggle about praying for their safety and my anger with God when the crisis occurred and I felt He had let me down. After explaining my own fears and what God showed me, I was able to further authenticate my faith for my daughters. They saw that even I grew through the experience. Today we all laugh about the Europe trip and the little car, affectionately named "Pepito." It's a symbol of a turning point in our family, I think—an awakening of independence and faith for all of us.

Our Tolerance and Grace

We see how important it is to our faith that we relinquish our lives to God first. We may experience circumstances that will tear at our hearts, but God will undertake to reach our children, perhaps in dramatic ways. When we're tempted to take control again, we should remember that we've already given our children as gifts back to God.

How do we point a child to God if that child has chosen to turn his or her back on God by abandoning his or her faith, refusing to attend church, or by embracing a cult or Eastern religion?

Will's college roommate was from India and was a Hindu. The two young men spent time together, and Will became fascinated with Hinduism. He started reading and exploring the faith, and at the end of the school year, he announced to his parents that he had decided to become a Hindu.

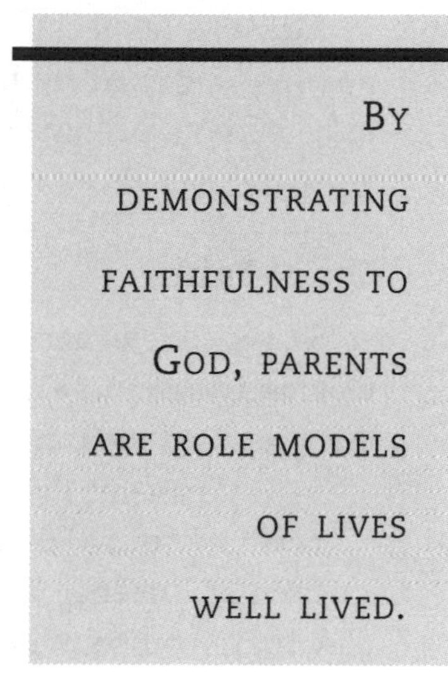

Horrified, his parents went to their minister, who wisely advised them to express interest in Will's new religion rather than condemn him for his new beliefs. He told them that college is the time when many young adults explore other world religions. They're developing their own self-identity, and religion is one area in which emerging independence is evidenced.

If parents are harsh and rigid, they lose the opportunity to influence their child's future thinking. The child will refuse to discuss religious matters with his or her parents, shutting the door to dialogue. On the other hand, if parents can be accepting of their child's freedom to explore other religions and will openly discuss the merits of other belief systems, they'll have the opportunity to share what they perceive to be the inconsistencies or detrimental practices of these religions. Open but noncondemning dialogue offers the potential to further influence the young person's thinking. By contrast, dogmatic, angry, explosive statements of condemnation shut down the possibility of future communication.

Parents often feel they've failed and thus give up hope. Yet nothing is gained by becoming downhearted. Parents need to be beacons of hope not only for children who have different values but also for the rest of the family.

Quiet Faith

Singer-songwriter Twila Paris in an interview with *Today's Christian Woman* magazine told some of the ways her parents demonstrated their upbeat faith:

> My parents always made us feel welcome. They were never too busy "doing God's work" to give me attention. Even as a teenager, I thought I must be the most entertaining company in the world because my folks loved to be with me—and with each of my siblings. It didn't occur to me until years later that they chose to spend time with us. Their public personas also matched their lives at home: their morning quiet time, passionate love for God, humble spirit.[1]

Some parents have forgotten, too, that adult children can change. Even when children have drifted away from the faith in which they were raised, loving parents will never give up but will pray continually. Most important of all, caring parents will remember that their strongest influence on their children is their own example. By demonstrating faithfulness to God, parents are role models of lives well lived. Consistent loyalty to God can be a powerful means of helping adult children return to the flock of the faithful.

Loving Acceptance Brings Change

Billy Graham's son Franklin was the perfect example of a rebel. In his book *Rebel with a Cause,* Franklin describes his rebellious youth and how his parents dealt with him:

> The sinful life I was living was not satisfying me any longer. There was an emptiness because my life wasn't right with God.

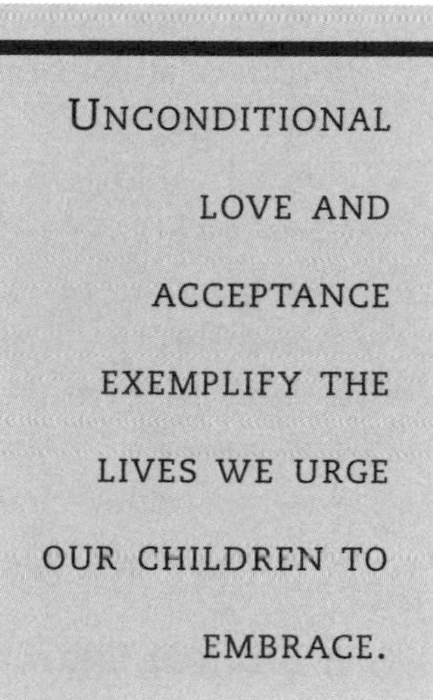

> During the Lausanne Conference I celebrated my 22nd birthday. Mama and Daddy wanted to take me to lunch.
>
> I chose a little Italian restaurant on Lake Geneva. It was pleasant and relaxed.
>
> After that, Daddy and I walked along a pathway beside the lake. My father, who hates confrontation, said: "Franklin, your mother and I sense there's a struggle going on in your life."
>
> I stared at him, caught off guard. *How does he know this?* I wondered.
>
> "You're going to have to make a choice either to accept Christ or reject Him. You can't continue to play the middle ground.
>
> "I want you to know we're proud of you, Franklin. We love you no matter what you do and no matter where you go. The door of our home is always open, and you're always welcome. But you're going to have to make a choicc."
>
> I felt angry. Maybe I was mad because he had seen

> right through me. I'd always thought I was so clever and could fool my parents. I couldn't figure out how he knew about the struggle that had been going on inside me for some time. But I knew he was right.
>
> After he had his say, Daddy patted my shoulder and smiled. He said nothing more about it as we finished our walk.[2]

This story has a happy ending. Franklin received Christ as his personal Lord and Savior within a few days and has been serving the Lord for the many years since. His parents' unconditional love, acceptance, and open door exemplified the Christian life we're urging our children to follow.

Again, we see in our dealings with our adult children a surrendering of our own desires for them. Even if we weren't following Christ when they were children or are new believers, as we relinquish them into God's care and set good examples now, continuing to pray, love, and accept them, we're paving the way for them to make right choices.

A Biblical Example: Jesus

There's no better godly example than Christ himself. Time and time again throughout the New Testament, we see Him setting the standard for our behavior. He loved sinners—reached out to them, in fact—in order to draw them into the kingdom of God. We see Him loving people in spite of their flaws, and ultimately, He made the greatest act of self-sacrifice by dying on the Cross for our redemption.

Parenting Pointers

In pointing your adult children toward God, you can take the following steps:

1. Surrender yourself to God first.
   - Pray for them and with them.
   - Share your own faith journey with them, even the weak areas. Be authentic in your faith by setting a godly example by your devotional time, forgiving when offended, praying for your enemies, exhibiting love for others.
   - Be led by the sensitivity of the Holy Spirit, especially in what you say to your children about their faith and the practice of it.
   - Pray about your goal of building a healthier, stronger relationship with your children.

2. Surrender your children to God, letting go of control for their lives.
   - Be noncondemning of their exploration of other belief systems. Be available to discuss the differences openly.
   - Love them unconditionally—without judgment, condemnation, or criticism.

3. Have faith in God's sovereignty. He's able to bring your child back to himself.

8

Loving Without Strings

Love . . . always trusts, always hopes, always perseveres. Love never fails (1 Cor. 13:6-8).

WE'VE all been to weddings and heard the "love verses" from 1 Cor. 13:4-8:

> Love is patient, love is kind. It does not envy, it does not boast, it is not proud. It is not rude, it is not self-seeking, it is not easily angered, it keeps no record of wrongs. Love does not delight in evil but rejoices with the truth. It always protects, always trusts, always hopes, always perseveres. Love never fails.

These are beautiful words, and we smile and nod when they're read during a wedding ceremony. But do we consciously practice these verses? More important, do we practice them with our family and our adult children? Consider the fact that love is not self-seeking. That means when you love someone, namely your child, you don't put your desires first—your wants for the right college, the perfect mate, or a high-paying career.

Do we keep a record of wrongs? Do we remember and remind them of past mistakes? Are we as patient and understanding with our children as we are with friends and co-workers?

Love Does Not Delight in Evil but Rejoices with the Truth

Patsy says, "My son is into alternative Christian music that most believers find offensive. He's in a band that wears black leather, multiple earrings, and has body piercings. But I don't criticize him for that. Why? Because he's a strong believer. With his music, he's able to reach countless young people who would otherwise be ignored by the organized church. I'm proud of him and support what he's doing."

Love Is Not Self-Seeking

Fred and Anita's son Jack had moved to another city about a 10-hour drive away. He had a fairly good relationship with his parents and asked them if he could bring his friend Marita home with him on the weekend his alma mater had a big football game nearby. He thought it was a fair request, but he was surprised to find his mother balked at the idea.

"We see you so seldom," she said. "I don't know, Jack."

"But Mom—"

Fred came on the line. "Son, we'll get back to you on this, okay?"

After they hung up, Fred and Anita talked. "Honey," Fred began gently, "I know you want to have the time with Jack to yourself. I would like that too. But we have to face reality here. He's dating Marita, wants to be with her, and we can say yes and have them both come or say no and take the chance he won't come at all."

"I never thought of it that way—I guess the loving thing is to be gracious to both of them," Anita said glumly.

Jack nodded. "Right. We want to keep our home always open and welcoming to him so that he *wants* to come."

> ARE YOU AS PATIENT AND UNDERSTANDING WITH YOUR ADULT CHILDREN AS YOU ARE WITH FRIENDS AND COWORKERS?

Jack and Anita recognized that trying to manipulate a situation to get what they want, which is more time with their son, could possibly backfire, leaving them with the opposite result. By not being self-seeking, by loving with open arms, they're promoting a healthier relationship with their son.

Anita could continue to grumble and complain that her son doesn't call enough or come to visit enough. We all know parents who heap this kind of guilt onto their adult children. Does this work? Do they get the results they want by trying to manipulate the relationship? I think we know the answer to that. It only serves to drive children away. Who wants to call home only to listen to whining about why we haven't come for a visit? No one. Instead, the child avoids going home altogether and less frequent communication results.

Agape is a Greek word describing God's love for us—it's "other-centered" and should always and forever be our goal. It's unconditional, putting others' interests first with no strings attached. That's how God expects us to love our adult children. Love is more than a feeling—it's the decision to act in a loving way.

It's important, too, to have hope that love never fails. Whatever the circumstances, choosing love is always the best, even if it doesn't seem that way. When our children hurt us—whether on purpose or unintentionally—we're supposed to forgive them. We can do that, but what do we *do* with our residual thoughts and feelings?

The secret is to learn to get rid of negative thoughts and emotions by giving them over to God. By cleaning out the "junk" in our hearts and minds, we're then cleansed and better prepared to let God's love flow through us toward our child—especially when we don't *feel* particularly loving. Love is, above all, a choice.

Love Is Patient; Love Is Not Proud

Paula and Ted learned more about how to love with agape love when their daughter Annette, always strong-willed, decided to seek design training in Los Angeles. Once she was on her own, Annette didn't seem to listen as eagerly to their advice.

She fell in love with a man of a different race. Paula and Ted knew that prejudice still existed, and they wanted to spare their child potential difficulties. They prayed about it, then told their daughter they would support the marriage if the young couple agreed to wait one year to test their relationship.

The couple agreed to wait.

Annette and her young man honored their part of the bargain, and Paula and Ted honored theirs.

The biggest problem was the young man's family. They did not approve of their son marrying a woman outside their race and fought their son's decision. They did not attend the wedding. To this day, nine years and two grandsons later, they do not support the union. But Paula and Ted chose to love their daughter and her husband.

In the end, Paula and Ted's time of soul-searching and listening to God produced an admirable choice: to practice agape love and receive their son-in-law into their family. They supported the marriage by surrendering what they perceived to be best to God's ability to lead their daughter. They embraced their daughter's new husband and today are reaping the benefits. They're proud and involved grandparents to their two grandsons.

Love Keeps No Record of Wrongs

Part of expressing love is clearing up any unfinished business or unresolved hurts. It's a good exercise to ask your children if there's anything you've done to hurt or offend them.

"I remember a talk I had with my older daughter about childhood, and she reminded me of a time when I had screamed at her, then punished her for what she considered to be a minor infraction," Marta said. "What my daughter didn't understand was that there had been reports of a man flashing young children in our part of town. I had told her not to go to the park after she got off the school bus, to come straight home instead. She disobeyed, and after waiting for her and then becoming upset and worried, I searched for her. When I found her at the park, I lost my cool. I admit it. I let my fear and anger erupt in a torrent of angry words. I remembered it; she remembered it. I asked her to forgive me for my harshness, which she did."

Extending grace is a big part of agape love. Just as our

Heavenly Father offers grace to us freely and without requirements, we should do the same. Grace can do much to bridge gaps in relationships, even when it's secondhand.

Secondhand Agape Love Works Too

Tim, now married and on the mission field, was once a rebel. His attitude toward his parents' faith changed dramatically when he witnessed their loving and forgiving spirit toward his older sister when she came home from college pregnant. He saw his sister receive sacrificial help and gentle guidance in place of condemnation. When she delivered her baby and returned to college locally, their mother watched the baby. His parents' love for his sister reached deep into Tim's heart as well.

Loving in Spite of Hurt

Some situations test our ability to love and extend forgiveness. Whether knowingly or unknowingly, our adult children can hurt us deeply. Maybe it's a consistent problem or something that just happened that needs addressing. First, we need to deal with our own emotions. If we talk to our child full of anger, the results will not be what we want. We will have vented, but our goal of strengthening the relationship will be thrown to the wind. Instead, we should tell the Lord how angry or hurt we are! Then we choose to give that hurt to Him by "taking our thoughts captive" (see 2 Cor. 10:5). Once we've done that and have forgiven our child for the offense, we're better able to confront the problem with a clear conscience. We're not all bound up in anger or resentment but have the desire to speak with love to air the situation, to keep focused on our goal: to promote a healthy relationship with our adult child.

Accepting God's Best

Learn to enjoy God's surprises with your children; they're much more interesting than your own small plans. Accepting God's best means giving Him complete freedom to shape your children for the calling He'll bring to their lives. Your part is to pray that they'll have a willing spirit when His direction comes and to let go with grace. One mom said, "There are many solutions to a problem, but anything other than love is only second best." We can love by listening empathetically to other parents, praying for their children, and offering genuine friendship. We don't have to counsel—just understand. We need not solve their problems—just pray for solutions and never criticize.

Bill Hybels in his book *Who You Are When No One's Looking* writes, "I have found that love is a lot more closely related to work than to play. It has a lot more to do with being a servant than with being a hero. When I set about the task of loving, I usually end up giving instead of receiving. Love inevitably costs me something, usually the three commodities most precious to me—my time, my energy and my money."[1]

Loving In-laws Without Strings

Often we must focus our love not only to our children but also to our children's spouses. We can express love behind the scenes by praying, even fasting for our children's marriages and for their spouses.

Anne explained, "My son and his wife are living in the

downstairs apartment in our home. My daughter-in-law doesn't handle criticism well and wants her way about everything. I've heard more than a few arguments, to say the least. Loving them by praying for them, and for her specifically, has been my only resource."

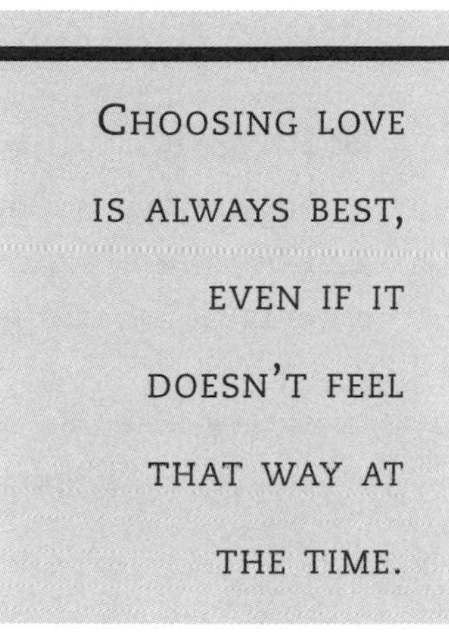

What if your adult child becomes involved in a homosexual relationship? Will being kind to his or her partner be saying you approve of the lifestyle? No—not at all. I would be willing to say our children know quite well where we stand on such an issue. Our unconditional love allows God's love to flow through us. This is not apathy or lack of concern; rather, it's choosing to love without strings.

How, you ask, do you show love to a homosexual child who comes home for a visit, bringing his or her significant other? Try to look beyond the sexual orientation and love the person. Be kind and courteous to the friend, but don't allow your child and the other person to spend the night at your home in the same bedroom. You should not have to endure behavior that puts undue stress on you. You have much to gain if you continue to respect, love, and demonstrate that love to your child. You'll be on the right track to gradually find ways to exert a more positive influence on your child if you keep the relationship open.

What's the alternative? If we berate and belittle our children for their choices, they'll probably be defiant and resistant. By digging in our heels, we're paving the way to pain and permanent separation from our loved one. This is an important time to remember our primary goal as parents: to maintain a relationship with our children.

Getting Out of the Way

How do we love without strings when our child chooses a mate we don't think is best for him or her, or he or she chooses to live in a homosexual lifestyle, or he or she abandons our faith?

These are examples of very emotional issues some parents face. We've taught, prayed, and talked about all these issues with our kids when they were teenagers. They know how we feel about these things, and now they're making choices contrary to what they know we would want for them.

First, it's important to remember that our child loves and needs us—still. He or she knows exactly how we're affected by his or her behavior. Our child knows that our continuing to be a loving parent does not mean that we approve of what he or she is doing or that we're violating our own values.

> ACCEPTING GOD'S BEST MEANS GIVING HIM COMPLETE FREEDOM TO SHAPE YOUR CHILDREN FOR THE CALLING HE'LL BRING TO THEIR LIVES.

So just as we've sought to give our child unconditional love in the past, regardless of behavior, we should also do the same now. We want to be a positive influence in the future, and this means we can't afford to break the relationship we have.

By choosing to practice agape love, we help with the wedding plans, even if we think it isn't the best match. It is, after all, our child's choice, not ours.

Leslie told me, "Our son dated a young woman for three years whom my husband and I loved. I assumed that one day she would be part of our family. Only that wasn't what happened. Our son broke it off with her, and when he began dating a young woman from another culture, I felt cheated, disappointed, and I knew, just *knew,* it wouldn't work. But my husband, Mike, reasoned with me, and we supported our son through the engagement and wedding, and now, through the birth of their children. God knew Anna would be the perfect match for our son—not the woman I had chosen for him. Getting out of the way and allowing our son to make his own choices by welcoming Anna into our family (even if tentatively at first), we have succeeded in retaining our healthy, loving relationship with our son and his family."

Love Always Hopes, Always Perseveres.

"'I don't think I want to see you for a while,' my daughter Jen curtly informed me," Alice recounts. "Her brisk, final tone signaled *Back off.*"

Hurt, shocked by her out-of-the-blue rejection, Alice got off the phone and had a good cry. Gently, the Lord reminded her that many of His children reject Him every day.

Months went by with short bursts of phone contact but little more. Lifting Jen in prayer would be Alice's only contact with her for a while as she immersed herself in career, a new housemate, and a move.

After several months, Jen phoned, inviting Alice to visit her new place. Praying to keep expectations low and guard against disappointment, Alice drove to Long Beach, California. Jen greeted her mother warmly. Excitedly, she began a show-and-tell tour of her new digs. Alice trooped after her, admiring her artistic flair. In the kitchen window box stood a stunning, slate-blue, glass-fronted memory box. It contained a black-and-white picture of Alice and her mother when Alice was a little girl. It was twined with silver French-wire ribbon and a blue-and-gold suspended heart.

REMEMBER: YOUR GOAL IS TO MAINTAIN A RELATIONSHIP WITH YOUR CHILDREN.

"Since my mother is a distant figure in my life, I didn't know what to make of the art," Alice said. "It seemed a chilling reminder, and seeing it in Jen's kitchen underscored our strained relationship. My daughter stood next to me, tipping her chin toward the box.

"'I made it for you,' she said.

"I stared at it, wondering what to make of this gift after the grief of her rejection.

"'It's beautiful, Jen—you're so talented,' I gulped.

"'Look more closely.' She gently lifted the box and placed it in my hands.

"Butterflies, apple pie, Irish boarding school—it astonished me that she remembered each one had special meaning in my life. I thought of the hours she had devoted to creating such a personal memento.

"I took her in my arms and felt tears wash away the sting

of rejection. Her love gift bespoke that near or far, I'm a part of her. In making the box, she said, 'I love you, Mother. I value your history and the things that are important to you.' The silver ribbon symbolized my daughter's love wrapped around my past and stretched into our future together. In receiving the box, I demonstrated my loving approval."

Again, what's the alternative? In not choosing to practice agape love, think of the consequences for us as parents. Think of all we'll miss in our children's lives.

Each of us has the ability to move beyond surface relationships—leaving behind meaningless routines, controlling behavior, or cold distances of the past and choosing instead actions that promote lively and nourishing interactions. It doesn't necessarily require more time than we spend together now, but it does take energy and creativity to transform the love we feel inside for our grown child into a palpable connection that will provide both of us with new strength and possibilities for growth.

A Biblical Example: Jesus

The best example of loving without strings is Jesus in what He did for us. He came to earth freely, suffered, then died on a cross for you and me. He had no personal agenda other than to see us reunited with God the Father. He gave His life to bridge the gap for us. It was selfless. It's love in its purest form.

Parenting Pointers

In loving without strings, you can take the following steps:

1. Commit 1 Cor. 13:4-8 to memory. Then *practice* it!

- Remember that agape love is "other-centered" love.
- Remember that love is not self-seeking.
- Remember that love is patient. Love is not proud.
- Remember that love keeps no record of wrongs. Forgive and be forgiven.
- Remember that love always hopes, always perseveres.

2. Know that agape love is more than a feeling. It's an action *choice*.

   - Agape is what God commands us to do in spite of our hurt and pain.
   - Agape is a form of service and obedience to God. It honors Him.

3. Recognize that it's never too late to start practicing agape love.

4. Know and believe that agape love will further your goal of a healthier, stronger relationship with your children.

9

Avoiding Friction Between Parents

Love is . . . not rude, it is not self-seeking, it is not easily angered, it keeps no record of wrongs
(1 Cor. 13:4-5).

OUR desire is to see our children become successful, independent adults, able to contribute to making the world a better place. But conflicts between the parents can arise—even quarrels to the point of separation, and in some cases divorce.

As individuals, we parents have our own ways of seeing things, of judging life's events. Our view is often tainted by the emotional baggage we carry from childhood traumas, broken homes, divorce. A plethora of reasons account for why we think the way we do. Add to the picture our spouse, who has his or her own spin on life, and voilà! Conflict arises, resulting in a shift of focus from our children to us, causing struggles that can traumatize a marriage and the family.

In dealing with parenting issues over the years, couples

often disagree over how to handle discipline, training, teaching spiritual principles—you name it. Yet somehow we've gotten to this point in time where our children are grown, and the problems are now bigger, more adult-sized, with more potential to harm or to have far-reaching consequences. In short, the pressure is on because the stakes are higher.

Above All, Present a United Front

Paula, mother of three grown children, says, "The main thing is the importance of unity and consistency as parents. It's normal and natural for a husband and wife to have different ideas, but they need to get all that 'talk' out of the way privately in order to provide a united front to their children, just as they did when the kids were younger.

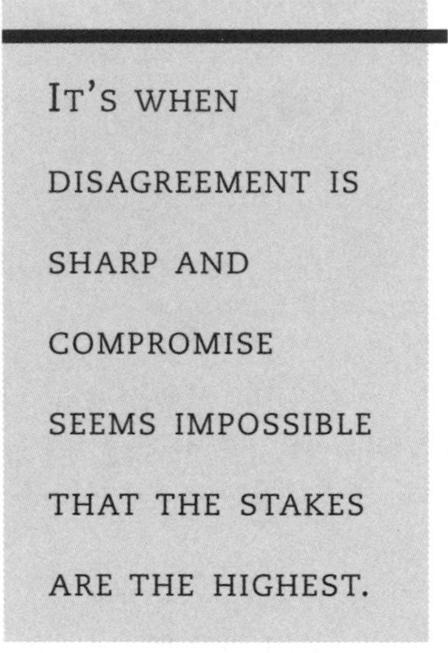

"I remember visiting my sister once when she and her husband kept bickering about some parenting issue in front of everyone. It created tension in their household and sent very mixed messages."

By thinking it through, you can buy time to weigh the options and consider all the angles. When asked for your opinion as a couple, you can present a united front by following these steps:

- First ask, "When do you need to know?"
- Pray for wisdom about the matter individually, and then together. "If any of you lacks wisdom, he should ask God, who gives generously to all" (James 1:5).

- After an agreed period of time, come together with your spouse and share insights.
- As you discuss the issue, express your differences to each other in private, negotiate until you find agreement, and then present a united front to your adult child.
- If you absolutely can't come to agreement, then don't offer your opinion or advice on the subject. Present a united front by being silent. Times when disagreement is vehement and compromise can't seem to be reached are often the times when the stakes are at an all-time high.

Unresolved Conflicts Can Result in Wrong Choices

In her novel *Atonement Child*, author Francine Rivers tells the story of a college student named Dynah, newly engaged to her "knight in shining armor." Dynah had everything going for her. Then one night on her way back to campus from work, the unthinkable happened—she was raped and became pregnant as a result. Her college asked her to leave. Her fiancé was devastated and broke their engagement. Deeply wounded and confused, she returned to her home in California.

There the problems escalated. When Hannah, Dynah's mother, told her husband, Doug, about the rape and the pregnancy, his reaction was emphatic:

> Leaning forward, he covered his face.
>
> "She doesn't want an abortion, Douglas."
>
> His head came up. "Well, she's going to have one whether she likes it or not."

Hannah stared at him, and he saw the disbelief in her eyes. "What are you saying? She has no choice?"

"You tell me what choice she has!" he said, angry, wanting to lash out. If the man who had done this to his daughter were to suddenly appear in the room, he would kill him—with pleasure.

Later in the exchange, their conflict continued:

"Lower your voice. She's upstairs."

He came closer, leaning down, jaw jutting. "If she refuses to have an abortion, people might even start wondering if it *was* rape. Have you thought of that? They might start thinking she and Ethan Turner went a little further than they intended."

He saw the jab hit home, watched it sink deep, twisting. Old wounds were ripped open, and she was bleeding again. "No, they won't. Not about Dynah."

"Yeah, right. Haven't you listened to the hens in our own church? They'd think it. They'd delight in thinking it—especially about Dynah. She can kiss her reputation good-bye."

Hannah watched him pace. "Are you worried about Dynah's reputation or your own?"

He stopped and turned his head, glaring at her. "What are you talking about?"

HUSBANDS AND WIVES SOMETIMES COME AT A PROBLEM WITH OPPOSING VIEWS ON DEALING WITH IT AND SOLVING IT.

Her eyes were cold. "Try this on for size: people would look at you as the father of an unwed mother."

"I can't deal with it, Hannah. I'm not going to—"

"Daddy—"

Douglas turned, his face going hot when he saw his daughter standing in the archway, a quilt wrapped around her. Her eyes were puffed and red from weeping. She looked at him beseechingly and then at her mother sitting hunched over on the couch.

"I'll go," she said in a choked voice. "I promise I'll talk to someone at one of those clinics. I—" She shook her head, her eyes spilling over with tears, her mouth trembling. She clutched the quilt more tightly. "Only please don't yell at Mom anymore—it's not her fault. It's not yours, either. I never meant to be a burden." Turning, she fled up the stairs.

Feeling sick with shame, Douglas stood silent in his family room.

Hannah stood up and walked slowly across the room without looking at him.

Douglas put his hand on her arm before she could pass. "Tell her I love her."

"Take your hand off me."

The coldness of her words struck him full in the gut. He gripped her harder, wanting to hold on to her, wishing just once she would understand how he felt about all of it. "I love her as much as you do."

Raising her head, Hannah glared at him. Jerking free, she walked away from him and went up the stairs.[1]

The events in this family were extreme, events we hope we'll never have to face. But they serve to illustrate how a husband and wife can come at a problem with opposing views on dealing with it, never mind how to solve it. In this illustration both parents had their own hang-ups from the past that played into their thoughts and decisions. Combine their hang-ups with the emotional nature of the crisis, and we see how they lashed out at each other, creating fresh, deep wounds. All this was in spite of the fact they shared committed love and an urgency for a better way for their child.

These parents were so far off course that their daughter was dragged along, forced to go a direction she didn't want to go.

Dynah was struggling to find the right way, struggling with all she had been taught by the very two people who were now at each other's throats. Needless to say, their mode of handling this crisis has only heightened the stress and frustration and crippled the decision-making process. There's an even greater problem raised here—will our conflicts as parents propel our children to make wrong choices?

As the story goes on, we see more of the impact their strained relationship had on their adult daughter.

Dynah escaped her parents' home to get away from the tension between them. She had come home to find guidance and comfort, but that's not what she found. Their strife over her situation only added to her confusion.

The negative effect of parental strife regarding parenting concerns is that our children suffer—the very thing we've worked so hard to avoid. Even if our adult kids don't hear our arguments or harsh words, they sense the problems. They're there, bigger than life.

If only Douglas and Hannah had done their talking in private first! If only they had come together, hashed it out, found some unity, or even kept silent in their disagreement, offering to help their daughter with whatever *she* decided, so much trauma could have been avoided.

Dynah eventually took matters into her own hands. She slipped away one night, leaving them a note, going off to fend for herself without the help of her parents. Instead of coming alongside her, her parents turned out to be an additional burden to her in her time of need. She was forced to make decisions alone, without their wisdom, input, or emotional support. The consequences could be irreversible and last a lifetime.

We're left to wonder if these parents made it intact or not. All we know is that they wounded each other deeply. It would be up to them to seek healing and restoration. It would be a long, painful recovery.

How often does this occur in families? How often do parents let their own differences, their own power struggles, and their personal emotional handicaps interfere with their lifelong job of helping their children?

Clashes Resulting from Emotional Baggage

Marlene is the mother of three young adults. She says, "It wasn't so much that my husband and I disagreed. It was more the dynamics of our intertwined relationships. I've never been too keen on any kind of conflict or confrontation. I was a classic 'peace at any price,' 'smooth things over' kind of gal. So when my husband had any kind of problem or misunderstanding with either daughter, I would swoop in to mediate and get things all patched up.

"In this process, my daughters would bring to me their problems with their father, and then I would go to him and attempt to intervene on their behalf. It was as if I were always defending one or the other of our daughters, trying to get him to understand them and listen to them. At other times, my husband would talk to me about a situation with one of them, and I would go to whichever daughter and try to help her understand.

"This practice created lots of friction and angst between my husband and me. After seeing a counselor, I realized the relationship between my husband and daughters was triggering emotional issues in my unhealed relationship with my father. I was trying to protect my daughters from what I had experienced. Without knowing it, I was making matters worse, almost guaranteeing perpetuation of the problem for another generation.

"To complicate things, my husband had a strained relationship with his mother that was also creating an emotional trigger for him. Unhealed baggage from the past impacted our current situation without either of us being remotely aware of it.

"I took responsibility for my part in the problem. I went to my husband and said, 'Honey, I know I've interfered in your relationships with our daughters in the past, and I'm sorry.'"

She went on to tell him that from now on she was responsible only for her own relationship with their girls. He would be responsible for whatever kind of relationship he had with each of them. Marlene would no longer mediate, interfere, or triangulate between them.

It was a hard habit to break, but she was determined. "More than once I bit my lip or left the room. On occasions I listened to either my husband or one of the girls vent about a particular problem but then encouraged them to go to each other and work it out.

"'It sounds like you need to share that with your daughter,' I would say, or 'It sounds like you need to talk to your dad.'"

Marlene prayed for them and stopped carrying messages back and forth. Over time, they began to resolve their disputes, and their relationships began to improve.

DON'T LET YOUR CONFLICTS AS PARENTS PROPEL YOUR CHILD TO MAKE WRONG CHOICES.

"And," she says, "the connection between my husband and me has become healthier and less stressful."

What's a Stepparent to Do?

Sheila and her husband, Derek, were affluent business people. They owned several businesses and lived in a beautiful home. They had no children except for Derek's two young adult daughters by a previous marriage.

Over the years, the girls came to visit on school holidays and summers. Everyone enjoyed their vacations together, shopping trips, and fun new electronic equipment.

Derek and Sheila footed the bill for expensive college educations, plane tickets to bring them home on vacation, clothing—you name it.

Sheila shared their problem with me. "Martha, this situation is so hard! Because we've been blessed financially, I'm beginning to feel like a bank teller instead of a parent. To say no to them—well, it feels stingy!"

"What does Derek say?"

ARE YOU LETTING YOUR POWER STRUGGLES WITH YOUR SPOUSE INTERFERE WITH YOUR LIFELONG JOB OF HELPING YOUR CHILDREN?

"He sees no problem with continuing to hand money over to them." Sheila shook her head. "What I'm seeing is a lack of gratitude from the girls. Any request they make, it's expected that we provide it. Yet they didn't even remember to send their dad a birthday card last month! I know it bothered Derek. It had to."

"Apart from that, giving them too much certainly doesn't help them learn the worth of their money," I said.

"It's really becoming a problem between us. They are, after all, *his* daughters. I've tried many times to suggest he say no. He refuses to listen, and it hurts. After all these years of being their 'other mom,' now I'm being shut out. It's definitely coming between us."

"Maybe this is one of those times to let go of your opinions and keep quiet," I suggested gently.

Sheila and I prayed and committed the problem to God, asking Him to speak to Derek about it. Sheila stopped offering suggestions and tried to let go of worrying about it.

For her, the potential for greater problems between her and her husband was diverted by relinquishing the problem to God. Being a stepparent has its own unique set of problems, and she wisely turned her focus to God instead of trying to persuade Derek to her way of thinking.

I haven't heard the final outcome about how Derek dealt with his daughters, but I know Sheila is feeling better because she's not so conflicted and torn apart. By praying for Derek and letting go of the problem, she's better able to have peace and harmony in her home while still maintaining a reasonable relationship with all her family members.

A Biblical Example: Galatians

The apostle Paul, in his letter to the Galatian Christians, talks to them about the sinful nature we're all born with. In Gal. 5:19 he describes some of the behaviors of the sinful nature: discord, fits of rage, selfish ambition, dissensions, factions, and envy. The list continues, all of which are actions that lead to friction and division.

Then in Gal. 5:22 Paul addresses the fruit of the Spirit of God: love, joy, peace, patience, kindness, goodness, faithfulness, gentleness, and self-control. Clearly, seeking unity and peace is a worthy goal.

Parenting Pointers

To avoid friction between you and your spouse, you can take the following steps:

1. It will help you stay focused on your child's needs if you do the following:
    - Surrender your own agenda.
    - Talk to your spouse in private first.
    - Agree to pray separately, seeking wisdom, especially if there's disagreement.
    - After an agreed period, join as a couple for prayer.
    - Come to a point of compromise.
    - If successful in reaching a compromise, only then speak to your adult child.

- If unsuccessful in reaching a compromise, maintain unity as parents by agreeing not to offer an opinion.
- Present a united front. Don't admit to your adult child that you disagree with your spouse.

2. Ask yourself if you're closer to your goal of building a healthier, stronger relationship with your children.

10

Renewing Married Life

Make my joy complete by being like-minded, having the same love, being one in spirit and purpose (Phil 2:2).

PSYCHOLOGIST Erik Erikson studied the phase of life after children are grown and concluded that it's a time when parents can move toward either integrity or despair. Parents can sink into depression or despair if they begin to feel disconnected from the people and relationships that once defined their lives. Integrity comes with finding meaning in life by renewing love and focusing on personal growth.[1]

Examining Individual Needs

When our daughters announced that they were moving to Hawaii together, I was excited for them. My husband was too. We encouraged them in this life adventure of exploration. We had been a military family, and thus travel and living in other places had been a big part of our lives.

The only problem now was that they were *leaving*—really leaving. I knew the hole in my life would be massive. Yes, of course—we'll talk on the phone, visit, e-mail, keep in touch, but it won't be like having them a few miles away. Those spontaneous shopping trips, movies, or dinners won't be happening anymore.

THE BEST THING WE CAN DO FOR OUR ADULT KIDS IS FIND CONTENTMENT AND SATISFACTION IN OUR OWN LIVES.

In preparation, I prayed about what to do with this new block of time in my life. Often the best thing we can do for our families is find contentment and satisfaction in our own lives.

I started watercolor painting classes again and established a stricter writing schedule. Yet I didn't want to simply schedule busyness; rather, I wanted to nurture myself in ways I had set aside or had never even thought about. With our children well on their way to independence, we as parents can now exhale and take time for ourselves.

My husband is doing the same thing, exploring new ways to grow. It's taken some time to recognize that it's actually okay to think about ourselves and our needs, individually and as a couple.

One man said, "My wife and I married at 20 and had our first baby at 22. The last baby came at 34. He left us when he turned 21. Why didn't someone tell us it would be 29 years before we were alone again as a couple?"

But what about situations and circumstances that require

more of us—infringing, if you will, on our time—such as involvement in child care, kids living at home, and so on? With the children finally grown, couples often discover that their marriage has stagnated. Added to that is the fact that parents can be portrayed as greedy, selfish, and insensitive when they focus on their own needs at this stage of life. How do parents get on with their own lives? Is it selfish?

Barbara and Jim had made plans to go to a premier showing of a new movie one Saturday night. Their son called Saturday afternoon and asked Barbara if she could watch his three children that night so he and his wife could go out. Barbara agreed, but when Jim found out, he was livid.

"Why did you do that?" he asked.

Bewildered, Barbara hadn't realized how much their outing meant to her husband. "I didn't think you'd mind," she stammered.

"I *do* mind! I think it's time we value *us*. *We're* important, too, you know."

Was this selfishness on Jim's part? I don't think so. In fact, this was their first step toward acknowledging that their relationship needed to become priority now that their children were grown and had their own lives. To constantly put your adult children first is to undermine your relationship with your spouse.

Author and teacher Dennis Rainey writes in his book *Lonely Husbands, Lonely Wives*,

> If marriages are to succeed and become havens of oneness rather than dungeons of isolation, Christians must do more than simply "add a few Christian touches" to the world's 50/50 plan. The 100/100 plan calls for a total change of mind and heart, a total commitment to

God and one another. This is the plan, the Super Glue, that holds a marriage together no matter what pressures may come.[2]

Making Oneness a Priority

John came home from work one day about four months after their last daughter had moved away. He found his wife, Jean, crying. She had had high hopes for this time of life. She always wanted to write, so she enrolled in a class at the junior college. She had many friends she wanted to renew relationships with, and she bravely told her husband that she had secretly signed up to take golf lessons so she could play golf with him.

None of this had materialized. Her English teacher was not enthusiastic about her short stories; her friends had their own lives and their own problems, and her golf drives curled out into the rough. She realized that all these plans were not very substantial. An emotional void had entered her life, a void that none of these things could fill.

When John heard her sobbing in their bedroom, he climbed the stairs two at a time and took her into his arms. As the story of her failure to adjust came out, he was patient and understanding. The next day he called his office to tell them he wouldn't be in that day.

He and Jean took a drive and walked by a creek. That weekend he cancelled his golf game with his regular foursome and instead took Jean to a driving range and helped her with her bad drive. Afterward they went out for dinner and talked and planned for their future.

Jean's depression lifted, and something else took its place. When John stayed home and gave her his weekend, it was not the time alone with him that was important. It was his attitude that neither his work nor his friends were as important to him as she was. She in turn responded to him with deeper tenderness. John was struck by what he had missed during the preceding years in their growing alienation. Together they planned each month to include more and more things that both had secretly wanted to do but that had not been possible when the children were around.

Making the marriage relationship a priority, as John and Jean did, is the first step. Get together with your calendars and set aside time for recreation, relaxation, and just plain talk. Reconnect by having fun together. Rediscover the things you used to do, and add new adventures to the list.

The freedom God gives us to become new is made clear in His Word: "Now the Lord is the Spirit, and where the Spirit of the Lord is, there is freedom. And we, who with unveiled faces all reflect the Lord's glory, are being transformed into his likeness with ever-increasing glory, which comes from the Lord, who is the Spirit" (2 Cor. 3:17-18). Who we become depends upon our acceptance of the changes and challenges God brings into our lives and how well we listen to His directives.

Time for Reevaluation

Virelle Kidder, author of *Loving, Launching and Letting Go*, writes,

> When Steve and I were on our own again after 25 years of dedicated, hearts-poured-into-it parenting, it felt wonderful! We had a future together, just the two of us. We were free to dream dreams, plan adventures, go fishing by ourselves, learn how to sail, write books, change

> careers, play the "oldies" loud, and eat the food we liked whenever we liked.
>
> We had rich years with our children, but it required sacrificing some of the richness of our time together as husband and wife. Now it had been given back—a gift from God, which we accepted with delight. Not only were our children free to become the adults God desires, but we entered the same freedom, as if in a dream, and it felt great![3]

We baby boomers are still young physically if not in years, and we have strength and vitality to explore life in new ways. Midlife with all its challenges often serves as a magnifying glass. It enlarges our view of what's truly important in life. The small things—a personal note, a hug, a listening ear, the sound of laughter, the smell of something tangy from the kitchen—all add up to a renewed awareness of the fragility of life and its wonder. It can also be a time of reevaluating priorities, assessing life's goals; it can be a window for change.

A Biblical Example: Caleb's Story

In Josh. 14:7-8, 10-12 we read about Caleb, a man unafraid of a challenge:

> I was forty years old when Moses the servant of the Lord sent me from Kadesh Barnea to explore the land. And I brought him back a report according to my convictions, but my brothers who went up with me made the hearts of the people melt with fear. I, however, followed the Lord my God wholeheartedly. . . . Now then, just as the Lord promised, he has kept me alive for forty-five years. . . . So here I am today, eighty-five years old! I am still as strong

today as the day Moses sent me out; I'm just as vigorous to go out to battle now as I was then. Now give me this hill country that the Lord promised me that day.

Caleb didn't just sit back in his midlife. He began a difficult and challenging mission at a time when others were nestled in their recliners planning early retirement. A sense of God's excitement about His purpose for his life kept him strong, positive, and vigorous. As you give God freedom to rebuild the tired, middle-aged person on the inside, a new you can emerge, one who says, *What's next, Lord?*

IT'S NOT SELFISH FOR PARENTS OF ADULTS TO GET ON WITH THEIR OWN LIVES.

Eccles. 4:12 reads, "A cord of three strands is not quickly broken." If a couple is united with Christ, they are automatically a cord of three strands. I'm seeing that the spiritual relationship my husband and I share is growing with more one-on-one time together. Often in the morning, while still in bed, we pray together—something we never had the time or energy to do in earlier years. It's intimate and relation-building to lie in each other's arms while we pray for the people and needs most important to us.

I find, too, that I'm praying for more understanding into my husband's heart. As we grow together, I'm more curious to see what makes him tick. I'm finding that I'm more in love with him than I've ever been.

All these things I've mentioned have arisen in my life because of more time, yes—but add contemplative time to that equation, and that's where the real meat is. In this stage of life, with our home consisting of just the two of us again, there's more time to think and ponder important matters. We meditate on God's Word, consider our purpose in this stage of life, where we're going, what we still want to give—the list goes on.

It's important to have a spiritual mind-set about aging; as our bodies age, we're being transformed more and more into the likeness of Christ. Similarly, it's important to nurture a spirit of giving and to be willing to adapt to the changes around us.

I remember hearing a few years back about the importance of finding new interests to share at this stage of life, because husbands and wives have often been so focused on raising their families that they've forgotten how to have fun together. Trying new things to see what we like is a way to bridge this gap. What are those things we've always wanted to try but never did? Make a list, and determine what you and your spouse are both willing to try.

Things you can do:

- Learn a new sport.
- Learn a new art or craft.
- Start a home business venture.
- Explore short-term mission work.
- Organize old photos, tools, and the garage.
- Make weekend plans or spur-of-the-moment plans.
- Volunteer.
- Take a class together.
- Buy season tickets.

My husband and I love to travel, and we take several vacations a year. The research and planning are a big part of the anticipation and fun we share. We've always been adventurous, and this is a way to continue exploring and making memories together.

Having a weekly date night is another thing we do. We take submarine sandwiches and head to the beach to have dinner and watch the sunset or go out for frozen yogurt and walk the bay. Our daughters may call while we're out, and when we return the call they seem surprised at our outings. My guess is they're thinking things like *You never did that when we were home!*

The best part of refocusing our attention on ourselves is our daily time to talk uninterrupted after my husband comes home from work and before, during, and after dinner. It's a relaxed time, and our sharing of details has deepened with no games to rush off to and no homework to help with.

Another big advantage to more uninterrupted time together is the ability to be as spontaneous as we were when we were dating and newly married. Oswald Chambers reflected in his book *My Utmost for His Highest*, "The characteristic of love is spontaneity. The springs of love are in God, not in us. . . . The evidence of our love for Him is the absolute spontaneity of our love—it comes naturally."[4] Often I'll call my husband and say, "How about we grab a quick bite and catch that new movie?"

Maintaining a healthy, vibrant marriage long after the kids are gone is a worthy goal that will affect our children's happiness for many years. Why? Because our success as marriage partners who place a high value on our relationship and strive to improve it will bring worlds of encouragement to our adult children. It may even be the reason they succeed.

Retirement Planning

Plans for retirement become a big topic of discussion when the children are grown. Many couples feel this time is one of "catching up" as they prepare more in earnest for later years. Airing desires, finding common ground, exploring opportunities as to where to live, and other such items are all part of joint planning.

Betty and Dan decided they wanted to retire in a more temperate climate than that of their New England home. So they started taking trips south, exploring various communities in different states. Finally they settled on a new community near the ocean, bought a condominium, and for several years leased the property out until they were ready to retire there. Their wise planning paved the way for an easy transition.

Our Kids Are Watching Us

One mother shared that her daughter told her that what she and her husband had done after the kids left home was really important.

"Mom, we've really been affected by the way you and Dad live your lives."

"What do you mean?" the mother asked.

"I mean the way you and Dad keep growing together, learning new things, branching out, and the way you love each other so much and do so many fun things together now. You're never boring. It makes us want to live like that too. It helps us not give up when things get tough. You two didn't."

Parenting Pointers

In renewing your marriage and refocusing priorities, you can take the following steps:

1. Accept the new circumstances in your life—your children are really gone.
   - Choose to grow individually. Give yourself permission!
   - Make growing as a couple a priority. How?
   - Honor your time together. Don't allow other obligations to subjugate your plans.
   - Be spontaneous! Have fun together.
   - Try new things.
   - Plan for your future together.
   - Encourage each other through this transitional phase of life.
   - Be understanding of each other.
   - Go out of your way to show empathy.
   - Cleave to each other in new ways.
   - Pray for new, deeper understanding of each other.

2. Recognize that having a strong, healthy marriage is a witness to your adult children that long-term relationships can be successful and rewarding.

11

Celebrating Your New Friendship

Make every effort to keep the unity of the Spirit through the bond of peace (Eph. 4:3).

IT'S hard work parenting a young adult. We want our grown child to be a responsible, independent adult. But above all, we want to have a relationship, a friendship even, with our child. We want to experience mutual respect and be available to listen, be a confidant, encourage, cheer him or her on. There are so many opportunities for animosity and dissention or for misunderstood intentions that ending up friends almost seems like an impossible expectation.

As with any relationship, it takes a certain amount of work to prevent misunderstandings, hurt feelings, and damaging disagreements. We always have to be careful with anyone we love to guard our precious connection. So it is with our adult children. How do we know we've reached that place of mutual respect and friendship? I think for me it was when I felt I didn't have to tiptoe and weigh each and every thing I said quite so carefully where my daughters are concerned. There's a certain ease that comes with a deepening friendship. There's a trust and belief that our priority is maintaining a good connection with the other person.

Yet I feel sometimes we fade in and out of this special place of friendship. For whatever reason, there seems to be an ebb and flow of understanding and good will. My hope is that underlying the ebbing times is a prevailing, firm belief that love is the driving force.

Seeking to understand what motivates another person can be challenging, but it's worth the effort to determine the whys of words or actions.

Friendship Is Possible

When I hear my friends talk about their relationships with their children who are ten years older than my daughters, I see growth and maturity in this unique friendship, and I realize I'm still very much in the process.

Margaret's daughters are well into their 30s. "Every time I'm with my girls, I get new insights into their lives, into their personalities, or I receive hints on how to do things in a less cumbersome, more efficient way. I'm finding as they mature they have much to teach me if I'll listen. I'm learning to allow more open-ended statements so our conversation can flow easily both ways. It's taken years, but now we enjoy a wonderful, mutual friendship. It was worth the wait."

Sometimes hints of a budding friendship appear in small, subtle ways.

While Deidre's grown son Mark was visiting her recently, he proudly showed her how to make doing laundry go faster. How? By filling the washer with water from a hose in the deep sink at the same time as the washer was filling itself!

The same son called Deidre one day at work, all excited, telling her about his "finds" of dishes and silverware—the kind that won't bend—for such a reasonable price. He was learning to appreciate his parents in new ways. Sharing his little discoveries was a new connection toward an adult friendship that made Deidre smile.

> IT SOMETIMES TAKES WORK TO PREVENT MISUNDERSTANDINGS, HURT FEELINGS, AND DAMAGING DISAGREEMENTS.

Veronica and Rich's daughter Lisa was an alcoholic, and after much turmoil in their family, she sought treatment and counseling. Through Alcoholics Anonymous, Veronica and Rich learned to detach from their daughter. In time, as Lisa worked on being faithful to her recovery, she and her parents became friends as they partnered in her process. Lisa saw her parents in a new light—as people who love her without judging her.

When Friendship Doesn't Happen

Our obligation before God is to raise our children the best way we know to become responsible and independent and then launch them into the world. While our goal has been to promote a healthy relationship with our adult children, friendship doesn't always happen. If that's the case, we still need to continue praying and seeking God on their behalf. Whatever the scenario, there comes a time when all we can do is rest in God's arms, knowing we've done our best. The task then is to simply wait. And waiting can be the hardest thing we're called to do. But the good news is that we're not alone in God's waiting room. He's sitting in the chair next to us, passing the time with us, never leaving us for a moment. So take heart, fellow parents, as we continue on this journey.

Our words, our experiences, *do* influence our children. They *do* matter. Maybe not right this minute, but ultimately they do.

Separation Can Be the First Step

How about those little moments that "zap" us with the recognition that a wonderful metamorphosis has taken place? Like a butterfly bursting out of its sheltering cocoon, friendship with Mom and Dad is something to be desired and sought out. I know, because that's what happened to me with my parents.

I think my separation from my parents zoomed the friendship process along. When I left my home in Boston at 19 and moved to Washington, D.C., with two girlfriends, I thought I knew so much more than my parents. We girls set up an apartment, started our civil service jobs with the Navy Department, and began the routine stuff of life. When I foolishly spent my whole paycheck on clothes and didn't have enough to pay my share of the rent or couldn't balance my checkbook, I called Dad. He laughed (not *at* me, mind you) and set me straight time and again. Slowly, I learned the responsibility and self-discipline I needed to make it in the grown-up world. In the process, my parents became my dearest friends.

In one of his monthly newsletters James Dobson wrote,

A brief update about our empty nest: My period of "mourning" lasted about thirty days, during which I didn't think I could take it. But guess what? Something interesting happened about that time: The new family constellation began to sound like a pretty good idea. The house stayed cleaner, adolescent noise and chaos gave way to serenity, and Shirley and I had much more time for each other. It turns out that God's plan is best after all. Now we enjoy a wonderful relationship with our grown children, not as parents who bear the responsibility for our kids' behavior, education, and training, but as friends who share an entirely new kind of bond that is just as rewarding as were the first eighteen years.[1]

Actively Building a Friendship

Meeting as friends can take some careful thought and effort when grown children live many miles away. You must put time and energy into improving relationships and creating activities that encourage mutual growth. Such activities bring the family together and leave everyone refreshed with a sense of vitality and belonging—and can be a challenge to find. But when you hit it right, family members say, "We should do this more often!" Everyone knows the competing demands of daily life make it difficult to get together as often as they would like, but if it's fun, everyone is eager to make the effort to meet again.

In Richard's family, the Fourth of July has evolved into a big family holiday. The event started out in the backyard with sparklers 20 years ago, but it's gotten so big that now it's at a park. As the years go by, Richard involves his kids and grandkids more in the production of the main event, a family talent show, getting their help to build a makeshift stage and decorate the area, as well as planning sporting events and contributing to the giant potluck. With the kids' help, Frisbee-throwing contests were added to the usual gunnysack races, and each year something new is added.

> KNOWING WHAT MOTIVATES ANOTHER PERSON CAN HELP YOU UNDERSTAND HIS OR HER WORDS OR ACTIONS.

Another family I know has a timeshare week at a resort in Hawaii, and they go together the same week every year. Their adult children know when to ask for their vacation so they can be with family and have rest and relaxation at the same time.

Paulette stays in touch with her family via e-mail; and every Sunday night at the prescribed time, they all get online, creating a "chat room." They'll spend about an hour telling jokes and exchanging news and plans for future get-togethers. Plus, digital cameras and Internet technology allow us to see our loved ones just moments after the pictures are taken, regardless of the distance between us and them.

Unexpected Benefits in the Family

My friend Jeanette shared about a recent outing with her two grown daughters.

"We try to meet once a week for a girls' night out. Usually we grab a hamburger and go to a movie, but this week we decided to linger over dinner. I sat back and listened to my two girls share about their lives, husbands, children, and schedules. A few short years ago, these two young women had little time for each other, but now—well, they have a lot in common.

PRAY FOR YOUR CHILDREN AND FOR YOUR RELATIONSHIP WITH THEM.

"We had such a good time, especially when we started laughing about their husbands' quirks. They weren't revealing any secrets, just sharing little idiosyncrasies that make the world go round. We're three women, very different but now friends.

"My heart swelled as we sat there enjoying each other. As a mother, I felt I had come full circle, and now my little girls were responsible parents themselves. I'm so grateful to God for giving us wisdom to get through the struggles with each one. Without His wisdom, we might not be here right now."

My friend Diane tells the following heartwarming story of her family.

"On Memorial Day, my husband, Bob, was on a ladder (in the rain). The ladder buckled, Bob fell to the ground, and he severely broke his leg. I called an ambulance, and we went to the hospital. Once we realized how severe his injury was, I called our sons to let them know and ask when we were done if someone could give me a ride home. (Our daughter and granddaughter were out of town). I told them it would be a while as the hospital was trying to get Bob a bed. Within 15 minutes of the phone calls, both my sons and one of my daughters-in-law were at the hospital. Not only did they check on their dad, but they also took me aside and inquired as to my welfare and then got me something to eat and a cup of tea.

"During the daytime I baby-sit our grandson and pick up our granddaughter from preschool. Jeff informed me that he had already made other arrangements so I didn't have to worry about it. This left me free to visit and help care for Bob in the hospital.

"Without my having to ask, my kids took charge. They called friends in to help out, offered rides to and from the hospital, called me every night to be sure I was okay, and helped out with daily chores. Even the little things around the house got done: the lawn got mowed, the trash was taken out, the dog was fed and cared for, milk appeared in my fridge, dishes were loaded into the dishwasher and emptied as if by magic.

"Our saga isn't over yet. Bob has had two operations thus far and may be facing a third. The kids are still all here pitching in and taking over some of the responsibilities that previously belonged to my husband or me.

"During this very stressful time, I became cared for like the child, and they became the parents, taking over, watching out for me. That's not to say I'm helpless by any means. But to have them take charge of the situation without my having to ask for help made me realize that they aren't children anymore. They've grown into fine adults and very good friends."

A Biblical Example: Ruth and Naomi

In the book of Ruth we read that Naomi and her family left Israel because of a famine. Her sons married Moabite women who were very different from Naomi. When Naomi's husband and sons died, she told her daughter-in-law

Ruth she was free to go back to her people. Ruth refused. They were bound together, and Ruth became dedicated to Naomi's God—the God of Israel. A strong friendship developed between mother-in-law and daughter-in-law, and together the two women returned to Israel. There Naomi set in motion a plan to reward Ruth for her faithfulness. Ruth married a kinsman of Naomi, and their friendship was sealed anew by becoming family through the marriage.

Parenting Pointers

To celebrate friendship with your adult children, you can take the following steps:

- Be available to listen.
- Encourage them.
- Cheer them on.
- Trust the friendship to God.
- Pray for them and for your relationship.
- Rejoice with them in their discoveries.
- Plan fun activities when they come to visit.
- Establish new traditions with their families.
- Plan a vacation every year or every other year with them.
- Use e-mail to keep in touch and send pictures.
- Discover online chat rooms for live discussions.
- Be willing students of the expertise and knowledge our children have gained.
- Affirm your adult children for their friendship.
- Thank them for their love and concern for you.
- Initiate!

Notes

Chapter 1

1. Mary Rae Deatrick, *It Hurts to Love* (Irvine, Calif.: Harvest House Publishers, 1979), 58.

Chapter 2

1. Anne LaMott, *Crooked Little Heart* (New York: Doubleday Anchor, 1998), 185.

2. Cliff Barrows, "A Conversation with My Dad," *Decision*, June 1994, 15.

3. Florence Littauer, *Personality Plus* (Grand Rapids: Fleming Revell, 1992), 24-27.

Chapter 3

1. Betty Frain and Eileen M. Clegg, *Becoming a Wise Parent for Your Grown Child* (Oakland, Calif: New Harbinger Publications, 1997), 14.

2. Liz Welch, "Grandparents to the Rescue," *Parade*, July 20, 2003.

3. Quoted in Virelle Kidder, *Loving, Launching and Letting Go* (Nashville: Broadman & Holman Publishers, 1995), 113.

4. Stephen A. Bly, *Once a Parent, Always a Parent* (Wheaton, Ill.: Tyndale House Publishers), 132.

Chapter 5

1. Ric Edelman, "Out the Door by Twenty-Four," *The Truth About Money* (New York: Harper Collins, 1996), 18.

2. Henry Cloud and John Townsend, *Boundaries* (Grand Rapids: Zondervan Publishing House, 1992), 46.

3. Ibid., 178.

4. John Rosemond, "Time for the Big Bird to Leap from the Nest," Knight Ridder News Service, *San Diego Union Tribune*, March 29, 2003, E.10.

Chapter 6

1. Joyce Brothers, *Parade*, September 1, 2001.

2. Gary Smalley and John Trent, *The Gift of the Blessing* (Nashville: Thomas Nelson Publishers, 1993), 225.

3. Gary Smalley and John Trent, *The Language of Love* (New York: Pocket Books, 1991), 42.

4. Ibid., 18.

Chapter 7

1. Ramona Cramer Tucker, "Twila Paris: Home for the Holidays," *Today's Christian Woman*, November-December 1994, 59.

2. Franklin Graham, *Rebel with a Cause* (Nashville: Thomas Nelson, 1995), 119-20.

Chapter 8

1. Bill Hybels, *Who You Are When No One's Looking* (Downers Grove, Ill: Intervarsity Press, 1987), 71.

Chapter 9

1. Francine Rivers, *Atonement Child* (Wheaton, Ill.: Tyndale House Publishers, 1997), 155.

Chapter 10

1. Betty Frain and Eileen M. Clegg, *Becoming a Wise Parent for Your Grown Child* (Oakland, Calif.: New Harbinger Publications, 1997), 143.

2. Dennis Rainey, *Lonely Husbands, Lonely Wives* (Dallas: Word Publishers, 1989), 54.

3. Kidder, *Loving, Launching and Letting Go*, 139.

4. Oswald Chambers, *My Utmost for His Highest* (New York: Dodd, Mead and Co., 1935), 121.

Chapter 11

1. James Dobson, *Focus on the Family Monthly Newsletter*, October 2002.